Children's Curriculum

Join the Kids HONOR ★★★★★★★ CLUB

I'm a member of the Kids HONOR ★★★★★★ CLUB

A Curriculum Guide
for Teaching Honor
to Children
Ages 3-12

Written to
accompany
the book and
video series by
Dr. Scott Turansky
and Joanne Miller,
RN, BSN

Publishers
Dr. Scott Turansky
Mrs. Joanne Miller, RN, BSN

Graphic Designer
Ellen Cranstoun

Editorial Team
Candy Fithian
Agnes Forker

Unless otherwise noted, Scripture quotations are from the Holy Bible, NEW INTERNATIONAL VERSION. Copyright ©1978 by the New York International Bible Society. Used by permission of Zondervan Bible Publishers.

Published in Lawrenceville, NJ by Effective Parenting, Inc.

Effective Parenting is a nonprofit corporation committed to the communication of sound Biblical parenting principles through teaching, counseling, and the publication of written, audio, and video materials.

ISBN # 1-888685-09-3
Printed in the USA
First Printing, January 2003

For information regarding permission or to find other resources for the family, contact:

76 Hopatcong Drive, Lawrenceville, NJ 08648-4136
(609) 771-8002
Email: parent@biblicalparenting.org
Web: biblicalparenting.org

Dear Teacher,

Through this curriculum it is our desire to equip you to teach children honor and to give them a vision for living life to the fullest. We have applied our education and experience to produce a children's program that grabs kids, teaches God's truth, and motivates them to positive change. We believe you will find this material easy to use, and a tool for growth in you as well as in the kids you teach. After all, children learn best what their teachers and parents model in life. We pray that God will richly bless you and the families you minister to as you all grow together in honor.

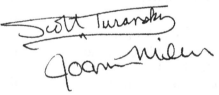

How to Use
This Curriculum

Teacher Note: You are now commissioned to teach one of the most valuable character qualities a child can learn: honor. After all, God thought it was so important, he added it to the Ten Commandments. We're not only talking about having good manners here. This is a study about a quality that will benefit children well into their adult lives.

Honor doesn't just make kids easier to live with, although it does do that. It prepares children for healthy relationships in the future. If you can help children catch a vision for honor when they're young, they'll make better students, employees, employers, and eventually will take honor into their own families as they get older.

But honor isn't just for kids. It's a quality for everyone to learn. So don't be surprised if you learn some valuable things yourself. Honor provides benefit to all our relationships. That's why we've included a devotional thought for you at the beginning of each chapter. Take some time to read it and pray that God will help you grow in honor as you teach the ideas to children.

Parent Note: This material is also designed to be used in a family for fun devotions or family night activities. Explain to your children that God commanded them to learn honor in families. Honor will make family life easier but more importantly it trains children to handle all relationships in productive ways. It's amazing how many things are learned through this one quality of honor.

Length of Lesson: Each session is designed to provide an hour to an hour and a half of fun and learning. However, the material can be shortened or lengthened depending on your needs. A family might choose to teach each lesson over 4 or 5 evenings. A Parenting Seminar Outreach children's program may last an hour and a half. The material was written with these options in mind. To lengthen each session you might add a story having to do with another character quality related to honor like love, patience, or generosity. Most people find that this curriculum offers more material than can be used in the time allotted. Choose the parts you want to emphasize. Don't feel you have to use it all.

Other Resources: Although this children's curriculum can stand alone, it was written to be used with the book, *"Say Goodbye to Whining, Complaining and Bad Attitudes, In You and Your Kids,"* and with the thirteen-part video series by that same name. In each 30-minute video the authors talk to families sharing humor, illustrations, stories, and drama to teach lessons about honor.

Order of Activities: Each lesson is divided into parts and is designed with children's developmental needs in mind. But children are all different and you may find it helpful to rearrange the lesson based on the needs of your students. As with all curriculum it's important to remember that you are not teaching material, you are teaching children. For example, you may choose to move the snack or the game to an earlier place because you sense the need for a change of pace during the session. So, know your lesson well enough to use it as a tool to give your students a vision for honor and a changed life.

Plan Ahead: Each lesson has craft ideas. Some require shopping, cutting, photocopying, or saving of supplies. Take a few minutes now and highlight the supplies needed and preparation section of each lesson. Make a shopping list or find helpers to prepare the craft supplies in advance. Working ahead may even allow you to add that little extra touch to make the craft special.

Contents

Join the Club

Preparing Your Heart to Teach Session 1:

Why do you think the Bible tells children eight times to honor their parents? It's even one of the Ten Commandments. Exodus 20:12 says, "Honor your father and mother." Obviously God thinks honor is a pretty important thing for children to learn. But honor isn't just for kids. The Bible uses the term honor over 200 times and encourages it in all relationships.

Did you learn honor in your own family as you were growing up? Some families have a greater ability to teach it than others. Whether your parents were able to teach you about honor or not, over the years you've probably learned that honoring others is one of the secrets to good relationships.

What makes an employee valuable? It's not just that he can do his job right. It's because he adds something more. His good attitude is contagious. He can see what needs to be done without being asked. He's an encourager. That's honor. The employer who finds a worker like that has found a treasure.

What makes a student stand above the rest? She doesn't just turn her paper in on time, but when the teacher looks at it he says, "Wow, this student did more than what's expected. I'll give her an A." Doing more than the bare minimum is honor.

The concept of honor helps children get along better in their families, but it will eventually help them to become successful employees, better students, better friends, and of course they'll carry these ideas into their own families when they get older.

As you teach this lesson, don't be surprised if you become more motivated to honor others yourself. Honor works. It changes people and strengthens relationships.

What Children Learn in Session 1:

Children are introduced to honor and its definition through a craft and activity. The idea of joining a club attracts children to the reality that some people choose to join in with honor and others don't. Special attention is then given to the fact that honor starts with learning how to treat people as special. The Bible story of Mary's special gift of perfume for Jesus and the Bible verse, Romans 12:10, communicate how important honor is to God. Children then get to play a fun game that evaluates different kinds of speech in order to practice looking for honor in life. The session ends with a brainstorming time to think of ways to treat family members as special this week.

> *...honor means treating people as special, doing more than what's expected, and having a good attitude.*

A Summary of the Video Session 1:

The concept of honor is introduced with a practical definition. **Honor means treating people as special, doing more than what's expected, and having a good attitude.** Parents are given specific suggestions for teaching children how to treat people as special. The session includes a story of how Scott's son, Josh, honored him with a special meal. Ephesians 6:2-3 is used. A spiritual application concludes this session asking people to consider their relationship with God as their Heavenly Father.
(parent training video series is optional)

Read Along in the Book, "Say Goodbye to Whining, Complaining, and Bad Attitudes... In You and Your Kids":

Pages 13-20 and 46-49 introduce the concept of honor and emphasize the part of the honor definition that teaches children to treat people as special.

Welcoming Activity

5-10 minutes

What children first experience when they walk into the room is important. Consider things like music, decorations, and a friendly greeting. Welcome them to the Honor Club. Invite them over to a table and encourage them to decorate a badge and a sign that say, "I'm a Member of the Honor Club." Patterns are available at the end of this lesson. Children can wear the badge by punching a hole in the top and hanging it around the neck with yarn, or by putting tape on the back and sticking it to their shirt. Children can take the badges home at the end of the session. You may choose to make special ones that they wear only while they are at the Honor Club.

★ ★ ★ ★ ★ ─────────────

Together Time

15-20 minutes

Use the thoughts and ideas below along with your own thoughts and the Bible to dialogue with the children and help them understand that honor means treating people as special.

Introduction:

As the children gather together, talk about the honor badges that they are wearing. Notice how they are decorated and praise children for their creativity.

Object Lesson:

Bring a bottle of perfume and spray a little in the air and ask children what it smells like. Do you like that smell? Why do people wear perfume? Because they want to feel special. Enjoy the perfume and offer to put a little on each child or have a couple different kinds for children to smell.

Bible Story with Application:

Read John 12:1-8 and use what you learn and some of the ideas that follow to tell the story to the children.

Once there was a woman who had some very expensive perfume. It was worth a lot of money. Maybe she even saved for a whole year to buy it. The story comes from the Bible in the gospel of John.

Jesus' friends had a special dinner just to honor him. Martha, Mary, and Lazarus each honored Jesus in a different way. Lazarus sat and talked with Jesus, Martha served the meal, and Mary gave Jesus a special gift.

Mary wanted to show Jesus how much she loved him so she put the special perfume right on his feet. I'll bet he had the sweetest smelling feet in the whole town, don't you think? Mary wanted Jesus to know how important he was to her. She was treating him as special. She was treating him with honor.

That's the name of our club, the Honor Club. Do you know why we call it that? It's because we're going to look for ways to treat people as special. That's what honor does. In fact, we say that honor does three things. It treats people as special, does more than what's expected, and it has a good attitude. We'll be looking at the other parts of the honor definition in other times together but today

we want to talk about ways to treat people as special.

Just like Mary, Martha, and Lazarus each found a different way to show honor to Jesus, you can think of fun ways to do the same thing in your family. What is one special thing that your dad does for you? What is one special thing that your mom does for you? How does that make you feel? When Mom or Dad takes you out to McDonald's or makes you pancakes for breakfast, that's treating you as special. What are some other things that Mom or Dad does to make you feel special? Are there some things that you can do to make other people feel special?

How do you think Jesus felt when Mary put the perfume on his feet? Imagine the perfume filling up the whole room. When we show honor it makes everyone feel good. But one man there didn't like the honor gift. The Bible tells us that he was a thief. His name was Judas and he had a problem in his heart so he didn't like the honor that was happening at that dinner.

Some people aren't able to be part of the Honor Club because they have some problems in their hearts. God wants us to get right with him and then to also show honor to others. One verse in the Bible tells us that honor is everyone's job. It's our special verse for today.

We're going to do a lot of things to show honor in this club but we each have to put honor in our own heart. It's not good enough to wear a badge. Honor isn't just something on the outside. It's something in our hearts.

Bible Verse:

Romans 12:10 "Be devoted to one another in brotherly love. Honor one another above yourselves."

Prayer:

Lord, thank you for the Bible and the stories in it. Help us to join the Honor Club in our hearts where only you can see. Amen.

★ ★ ★ ★ ★

Craft and Activity Time

15-20 minutes

Fishing for Honor

Supplies:

- One unsharpened pencil for each student
- A piece of yarn about two feet long for each child
- A 1/2 inch button magnet for each child
- Photocopy of fish onto card stock (see the pattern at the end of this chapter)

Preparation:

Attach a magnet to a piece of yarn for each child. Hint: Wrap the string around the magnet a few times and then use a glue gun to put a dab of glue to hold in place. Or, wrap the magnet in a small piece of tissue paper and tie the yarn around the loose ends of the tissue paper that are bunched up on top and secure with a dab of glue. For younger children you may want to cut out the fish. Older kids can cut out their own fish as part of the activity.

Give children three fish to color, each one having a different part of the honor definition. You'll want to tie the strings to the "pole" for the

younger children. The older kids can fasten their own string to the pole. Each fish needs a paper clip fastened through the hole.

Activity

Create a "fish pond" by placing the decorated fish on the table or floor with children in groups of three or four. Children enjoy "catching" the fish with the magnet. You might start by letting them play while you talk about the honor definition. Then you could try one or more of these ideas:

- Children must catch one of each but only one of each.

- Children must catch

Game

15-20 minutes

"Whoops and Aaah" game. Tell children that words can be honoring or dishonoring. Read each of the following statements asking children to respond by saying either "Whoops!" or "Aaah."

> **Your shirt looks ugly.**
> **I don't want you to play with me.**
> **I like you.**
> **Would you like to share my markers?**
> **I want the first piece.**
> **You can't have any.**
> **Thank you for sharing that with me.**
> **I'm the fastest runner in this room.**
> **You can't do it right.**
> **I like that dress.**
> **No, I don't want to share.**

Have children think of some other "Whoops" and "Aaah" statements. Ask them for ideas.

one of each but all on the same pole. If they catch more than one of a kind, they must throw them all back and try again.

- Children keep playing until they have caught one of each.

- Children take turns fishing, watching each other catch fish.

While children are playing with this activity remind them about the Bible verse. You might say things like, "Our Bible verse today says, 'Honor one another above yourselves.' What are some ways we can show honor. They're written right on the fish." Have children leave their fishing poles and fish on the side of the room where they can retrieve them later so that they won't be distracted by them as they continue with the activities.

To help you might give some situations such as these. Brainstorm both honoring and dishonoring statements, have the group respond with a "Whoops" or "Aaah" to each suggestion.

- If you want a snack, you might go into the kitchen and say, _____.

- If someone has taken your seat you might say, _____.

- If someone trips and falls you might say, _____.

- If you make a mistake you might say, _____.

- If someone does something nice for you, you might say, _____.

- If Mom tells you to pick up the toys, you might say, _____.

Here is a suggested dialogue to use as part of the "Whoops" and "Aaah" game. You might read this story and pause for children to respond, or, with

older children, you might photocopy this page and choose two people to each say a part and others to respond to what they hear.

Matthew: Hey Susan. I really like that picture you drew. You're a good artist.

Susan: Well, it's about time you said something nice about me. (sarcasm)

Matthew: I say nice things all the time. You just don't listen. (arguing)

Susan: I'm sorry, that really was something nice for you to say to me. Will you forgive me?

Matthew: Yes, I forgive you.

Matthew: Did you like the story I told in Sunday School today? I'm a great storyteller. In fact, I'm good at everything I do. (boasting)

Susan: Well, you really are good at telling stories.

Matthew: Yeah but then I had to help the teacher clean up after craft time. What a mess! (complaining)

Susan: I like to help our teacher. I never complain. (boasting)

Matthew: Well, you are a good helper.

Susan: Thanks Matthew, you're a good friend.

Snack

5-10 minutes

Bake some homemade cookies, cupcakes, or other special treat and talk about how you wanted to honor the children by treating them as special. Bring out the treats and talk about the delight you see on children's faces. Use the opportunity to talk about their favorite foods that Dad makes or Mom makes and how Dad and Mom treat them as special by buying or cooking these things.

Review and Close

5-10 minutes

Ask children to repeat the honor definition. See who can say all three parts. Ask children for ways that they might treat someone as special in their family. Who will you try to treat as special this week? What are some ways you can do that? You might suggest some of the following:

When someone does something nice to honor you like making a meal or taking you somewhere, you can honor them by saying thank you. You can treat someone as special by giving a hug or a smile. You can say, "I love you." You might do something nice to surprise Mom or Dad. Ask children for some ideas for showing parents or siblings that they are special.

Welcome children again to the Honor Club and tell them you'll be eager to hear back next time how they're doing at showing honor to others. Pray and ask God to remind us all to show honor this week.

Instructions:

Photocopy this page onto heavy paper or card stock and use it according to the instructions in this lesson.

I'm a
member of the

Kids HONOR
☆ ☆ ☆ ☆ ☆ **CLUB**

Treating People as
Special ○

Doing
○ **More**
than What's
Expected

Having a
Good ○
Attitude

HONOR CLUB

I'm a member of the **Kids HONOR CLUB**

Are You a Drain or a Fountain?

Preparing Your Heart to Teach Session 2:

When was the last time you received a surprise? Don't just think about the big surprises like a birthday gift, but think of the little ones, like an unexpected thank you or an encouraging word from someone you appreciate. It's those little surprises in life that give a real lift to your day. Honor does the same thing. It gives more than what's expected. It adds energy to relationships and the result is delight.

Try a little experiment. Several times today, give little unexpected gifts of kindness and watch what happens. Give a small gift here, a patient response there, let someone go in front of you, or encourage someone with a compliment. Watch the smiles and other pleasant responses on the faces of people. Those are all examples of ways to show honor. People are delighted and you experience the value of honoring others in little ways.

In the sermon on the mount in Matthew 5 Jesus made several statements about the value of doing more than what's expected. In verses 38-39 he says, "You have heard that it was said, 'Eye for eye, and tooth for tooth.' (That's what expected.) But I tell you, Do not resist an evil person. If someone strikes you on the right cheek, turn to him the other also." (That's doing more than what's expected.)

Jesus talked about the benefits of giving a little extra to others. He talked about going the extra mile, turning the other cheek, doing your acts of righteousness in secret, and blessing your enemies. These are all examples of honor. God loves honor and even rewards those who give it to others. Honor not only benefits others but it changes the giver and makes him or her more enjoyable to be around.

Much is said today about a person's IQ but how is your HQ? HQ stands for Honor Quotient. Your HQ says a lot more about you than intelligence ever could. Those who are most successful in life have learned a valuable lesson already—the importance of honoring others.

What Children Learn in Session 2:

Some children have the ability to drain the energy right out of family life. In this session children learn that honor means doing more than what's expected. They make an honor poster to help reinforce the honor definition. They also hear a Bible story about a little girl who did more than what's expected and helped her master's husband get well. Children are challenged to look for ways to add energy to family life by doing more than what's expected.

A Summary of the Video Session 2:

Introducing this session, Scott tells the story of Mike who learns a surprising lesson by doing more than what's expected. Children are taught how to add energy back into family life instead of draining it. Practical suggestions are given for teaching children to do more than what's expected. Ideas include honoring others while setting the table, the importance of cleaning the corners, not just getting by, and how to show honor when you leave the bathroom. Matthew 5:38-45 is used. Four suggestions for dealing with a bad attitude are also presented.
(parent training video series is optional)

Read Along in the Book, "Say Goodbye to Whining, Complaining, and Bad Attitudes... In You and Your Kids":

Pages 49-55 teach the importance of doing more than what's expected and having a good attitude.

Session 2

Welcoming Activity

5-10 minutes

As children come in, welcome them and invite children to the table to decorate their own Honor Poster. Young children may not be able to read the poster but will still get the idea and appreciate decorating it and taking it home. Photocopy one for each child onto heavy paper or card stock and allow the children to color their page with crayons or markers. As an added touch, mount the page on construction paper. You may even want to allow the children to decorate their posters with glitter or stickers. They might also draw some pictures around the edges of ways to show honor. Encourage the children to take their posters home and hang them in special places.

Together Time

15-20 minutes

Use the thoughts and ideas below along with your own thoughts and the Bible to communicate the fact that honor means doing more than what's expected and adding a little extra to family life.

Introduction:

Welcome children back to the Honor Club. "Can anyone tell me what honor means?" "Did you find ways this week to treat people in your family as special?" Have several children share. "Did anyone treat you as special?" "I can tell you liked that. That's honor."

For Older Children: "Can you think of phrases with the word 'honor' in them?" A few examples might include Honor student, seat of honor, a judge is called Your Honor, on my honor expresses integrity, and honorable mention. "Let's look at the Honor Poster you made." Recite the honor definition and ask children where they are going to put their honor poster to remind them to show honor to others. Reveal that next week they are going to get another poster with a different quality on it. Encourage them to put these posters up in a special place as a reminder.

For Younger Children: Have fun showing happy faces when we're delighted. Have them frown until you say, "I like you," or "Let's go out to dinner tonight." Talk about what a happy face looks like and how honor makes a face glad.

Object Lesson:

Blow up a large balloon to a medium size. Let air out or put more air in as you say something such as: A family is like this balloon. It takes a certain amount of air to make things work smoothly. Some people in a family drain energy out of family life. They don't do the right thing; they continually think only of themselves, they leave messes all around. They drain energy out of family life (let little bits of air out of the balloon).

Then there are those that add energy to family life. These people do extra things to make the family better. They show honor. They help clean up messes, they talk nicely to one another, they cooperate and smile (blow balloon up more in little spurts). Those families have a happier life. Continue to add or remove air from the balloon as you ask the following questions. "Are you the kind of person that adds energy to family life or someone who takes energy out of family life?"

Talk about a few examples of things that drain energy out of a family like whining, complaining, arguing, or being mean. Suggest some things that add energy to family life like saying please or thank you, helping Mom set the table or Dad carry in the groceries.

Bible Story with Application:

As you prepare, read 2 Kings 5. Use some of the following thoughts to tell the story in your own words.

Naaman was the general of a big army. He won many battles and was a great man but he had a problem. He had leprosy. Leprosy is a disease that gives you sores on your skin. It was very sad because there was no way to get rid of the leprosy.

Naaman's wife had a little servant girl who worked for her. Every day the little girl would do chores and get things done around the house. She knew that Naaman was sick and that he was worried that he wouldn't get well. The servant girl knew about a prophet, Elisha, who could heal people. The little servant girl knew that if Naaman went to Elisha, God would do something great.

What should she do? Should she just do her chores and think about the things she needed to do around the house, or should she help Naaman? It reminds me of some of the choices children make in their own homes today. Should I go play or should I pick up these dirty clothes in my bedroom? Before I go read a book should I take this dirty bowl and glass to the kitchen? Some children don't even see those things. All they think about is themselves. That's sad. They don't add energy to family life. They just take it away like in our balloon. Then other people like Mom or Dad have to do extra work. How do you think that makes them feel?

Well the little servant girl decided she would help. That was a very important decision. She went to Naaman's wife and told her about Elisha the prophet and how God could heal Naaman. When Naaman heard this good news, he went to his commanding officer and asked for permission to go talk with Elisha. The commanding officer said, "Yes," and gave Naaman some official papers to take with him.

When Naaman arrived at Elisha's house, he was excited because he thought, "Elisha will heal me and I will get rid of this leprosy." But it didn't happen that way. Instead, Elisha gave Naaman a dirty job to do. He told Naaman to go and wash himself in the dirty Jordan River. Naaman didn't like that idea. After all, he could think of the clean river near his own house. Why should he go and do this dirty job? Can you think of some dirty jobs around your house?

How about scraping dishes or washing out the dog bowl or cleaning the toilet? Are you big enough to do the dirty jobs or do you only do the easy ones? If you want to add energy to family life, sometimes you do the difficult or the dirty jobs. It requires a servant heart. We call it humility. Wouldn't your dad or your mom be surprised if you cleaned up a dirty mess without even being asked?

Naaman's servants encouraged him to listen to Elisha and to wash in the Jordan River. So Naaman did the dirty job just as Elisha said. Actually Naaman had to dip himself in the dirty water seven times. That's a lot of times to get dirty. On the seventh time, Naaman came up out of the water and his leprosy was gone. God had done a miracle. Naaman was so happy. I'll bet he was glad that his servants and the little servant girl had helped him. He was now well. That little girl didn't just think about herself. She did more than what was expected and God used her in an exciting way.

Sometimes we do things that add to family life and nobody even notices. But God notices. Here's our Bible verse for today.

Session 2

Bible Verse:

Matthew 6:1, 4 "Be careful not to do your `acts of righteousness' before men, to be seen by them…Your Father, who sees what is done in secret, will reward you."

Talk about the Bible verse and ways that children can do more than what's expected. Challenge the children, as members of the Honor Club, to look for ways to do extra things at home that need to be done. Help them see that even if no one notices, God does, and he loves honor. God invites people to be part of the Honor Club in their own lives and one way that you show that you're in the club is by doing more than what's expected.

Prayer:

Lord, please help us this week to think about more than just our own selves. Teach us how to see things that need to be done and ways that we can add to family life. Help us to be like the little servant girl and do more than what's expected. Amen.

★ ★ ★ ★ ★

Craft and Activity Time:

15-20 minutes

Honor Party Favors

Supplies:

- One cardboard toilet paper tube per child
- Squares of paper and pencils or markers to write notes
- Precut squares of wrapping paper or white paper that children can decorate with markers
- 2 pieces of yarn for each child, 12" each
- Individually wrapped pieces of candy

Have children make an honor "Party Favor" gift for their family. Provide a cardboard toilet paper tube for each child. The children can fill these with candy and notes. Have small pieces of paper so the children can write something nice about each family member. The candy and the notes go into the tube and then the child can wrap it with wrapping paper and tie each end with yarn. Younger children can draw small pictures instead of writing notes. Notes might say things like, "I like my family." "My family is special." "Our family makes a great team." etc. Explain to children that honor means doing more than what's expected. Help them anticipate the delight others may feel when the party favor is revealed at a special time this week. Encourage children to give their gifts to the family at a mealtime when everyone is together.

Activity

For Young Children: Bring a laundry basket full of unfolded towels and have the children help you fold the laundry. (This activity has been fun for the children and it's amazing how many parents later report that their children wanted to help with the laundry at home.) Talk about doing extra around the house as you work together.

For Older Children: Hand out the "The Honor Challenge" sheets (photocopy one per child from the master at the end of this lesson.) Ask children to write in the first box a list of the chores they do at home. In the second box, list several things they might do that are extra, unexpected things. You might encourage children to fill in the blank, "My mom would sure be surprised if I…" Or, "My dad would be delighted if I…" After listing several ideas in this box, encourage children to take "The Honor Challenge" sheet home and write down things in the last box that they do during the week to show honor. Ask them to bring the sheet back next week to report.

Game

15-20 minutes

Balloon Volley Ball

This game is appropriate for all ages. Divide the group in half with each group on opposite sides of the room.

Have two leaders or children hold up a rope or extension cord as a

net about four feet off the ground. Have the children play volleyball with a balloon, being careful to allow several children to participate.

It's best to not limit the amount of hits per side. Look for honoring comments and actions on the part of children. Discuss ways that children can help others have fun, thus making it fun for all.

★ ★ ★ ★ ★

Snack

5-10 minutes

Provide "Energy Bar" type snacks. They might be individually wrapped granola bars or home made cookies shaped like an energy bar. Talk about how these snacks provide energy to get you going. Food does that for the body. Honor adds energy to the family. Talk about how important energy is in both situations.

Review and Close

5-10 minutes

What's the difference between a fountain and a drain? Some kids are fountains in a family and some are drains. Which one are you? How do you know? How can others tell?

Talk about things we do in the family for each other and things we can do in secret such as cleaning, surprises on someone's pillow, doing the dishes, etc.

For Older Children: Brainstorm with a list on a white board or large pad and easel. You can do this as a large group or break into smaller groups and then have them report to the larger

group. Ask children to suggest something they might do and encourage them to come next time and report back.

"Do you remember the balloon illustration from earlier? What did that show us?" Remind children that some kids drain energy out of family life and some add energy back into the family. "One way that people drain energy out of a family is with a bad attitude. What does a bad attitude look like?" Encourage children to show a pouting face, angry posture, mouth noises, walking with a bad attitude, etc. Have children role play situations in family life where one is the parent and the other is a child with first a bad attitude, and then a good attitude. The "parent" may make a request to clean up the clothes on the floor or come and set the table. Have a fun time with this and you'll illustrate a common pitfall in family life.

Be sure to end with suggestions that children look for ways to add energy to family life this week and report back to share some of their ideas.

Instructions: Fill in the first two boxes out now. During the week add things to the bottom box. Bring the completed sheet back to the next meeting of the Honor Club.

Name: _____

My Chores and Responsibilities

Ideas of Things I Could Do This Week to Show Honor

Extra Things I Did This Week to Show Honor

HONOR

- **Treating people as special**
- **Doing more than what's expected**
- **Having a good attitude**

Who Likes a Whiner?

Preparing Your Heart to Teach Session 3:

When are you most tempted to whine or complain? Is it when you have to wait in traffic or are stuck in a slow line at the store? Or maybe you're tempted to join in when you hear others complaining about the weather, politics, or taxes. Whining and complaining are honor issues and have to do with the way we look at and react to problems.

We all experience negative things in life but not all people respond by complaining. Some people need just a little nudge and they're off and running, moving into the whining and complaining mode before they even realize it. It's always encouraging to see those who have an amazing ability to look past the problems of life to solutions, or they focus on the things they're grateful for, or they try to encourage others under pressure.

Christians would never claim to be atheists, but sometimes they live like practical atheists –as if God doesn't exist. Next time you find yourself under pressure or tempted to complain, ask yourself how your faith changes the way you respond. Philippians 2:13-14 ties our faith to our everyday responses. It says, "It is God who works in you to will and to act according to his good purpose. Do everything without complaining or arguing."

Honor works even in difficult situations. In fact, as with most character, pressure is the real test. As you help children grow in honor this week, be on the lookout for ways you might also apply honor under pressure. You'll be surprised at how a little work on honor can help you become an encourager instead of a whiner.

What Children Learn in Session 3:

Some children can't seem to receive any instruction or correction without complaining. In this session children will learn the definition of obedience as well as alternatives to whining and complaining. They will tape record their own voices whining and complaining and then listen to themselves. They'll also hear about what happened to the Israelites when they seemed to whine and complain about the same things kids complain about today. Whining and complaining are not honoring. In this session children will learn two honoring alternatives.

A Summary of the Video Session 3:

Whining and complaining are dishonoring. Children are taught that there are two kinds of people in the world, whiners and solvers. Whiners focus on the problem. Solvers concentrate on the solution. Two biblical alternatives are presented for whining and complaining. "Obey first and then we'll talk about it" is illustrated in scripture with people like Abraham, Peter, and Philip. A "wise appeal" is illustrated through the life of Daniel, Esther, and Nehemiah. Parents learn how they sometimes contribute to their children's whining and learn several practical ways to address it.
(parent training video series is optional)

Read Along in the Book, "Say Goodbye to Whining, Complaining, and Bad Attitudes... In You and Your Kids":

Pages 25-43 talk about the difference between obedience and honor. It's not enough to get your children to do what you ask. The way they do it is also important because that's where honor is demonstrated.

Welcoming Activity

5-10 minutes

Make an Obey Poster

Use the Obey Poster at the end of this lesson. This page complements the Honor Poster that the children did in the last session. Have a copy for each child and allow the children to color their page. Then mount the pages on construction paper. You may even want to allow the children to decorate their posters with glitter or stickers. They might also draw some pictures of obeying around the edges. Encourage the children to take their poster home and hang it in a special place.

★ ★ ★ ★ ★

Together Time

15-20 minutes

Use the thoughts and ideas below along with your own thoughts and the Bible to dialogue with the children and help them understand that whining and complaining are not honoring.

Introduction:

Teach children the Three Finger Rule. As you show each the three fingers the children respond accordingly. First finger up, then everyone is quiet. When the second finger goes up, everyone smiles, and with the third finger up, everyone sits up straight. It's a fun way to teach children some class rules.

At the last session children had an assignment to do more than what's expected and report back. Ask them if they can think of ways that they did more than what's expected and if they thought of other ideas of ways they can add energy to family life. Ask children where they hung their Honor Poster last week and where they are going to hang their Obey Poster this week. Go over the Obey definition a few times. Obey means to "do what someone says, right away, without being reminded."

Object Lesson:

Bring a tape recorder and record the children whining and complaining. "What does whining sound like? What does complaining sound like when you don't want to clean up the toys? Let's all whine at the same time?" Allow children who are particularly good at it to whine alone into the tape recorder. After a few minutes of taping, play it back for the children to listen to what whining sounds like. Have a fun time laughing at the whining voices.

Bible Story with Application:

Read Exodus 16-17 and use the things you learn and some of the thoughts that follow to tell the story to the children, teaching them that whining and complaining are not honoring.

The Israelites had traveled a long time. I'm sure the children were whining and saying, "Dad, are we there yet?" (whiny voice) That's what kids do on long trips sometimes. They began to complain and say things like, "I wish I didn't have to go on this trip." And "I wish I were back home." (complaining voice). Did you ever take a long trip like that and wish it would get over quickly?

Then they got hungry and started complaining about

that. They said, (whiny voice) "I'm starving." "I'm hungry." "I want to eat at McDonald's." Well actually they didn't say that last thing because there weren't any McDonald's around. They were out in the desert. There was no food. The people were sad and they were doing a lot of complaining about it.

God decided to do a miracle. He loved the Israelites so much and he wanted them to be happy so he had flour fall down from heaven at night while they were sleeping. In the morning they could go around and gather the flour up and they had something to eat. Everyone had just enough. When the people first saw the flour, they didn't know what it was so they called it "Manna" which means, "What is it?" in Hebrew. Then they used that flour to make all kinds of recipes. I'm sure they made manna pancakes and manna waffles and manna biscuits and manna cookies. They probably made rolls and loaves of bread. They loved that manna. It was great. God also gave them meat to eat in the evenings.

God didn't want the people to be selfish so he told them not to save any when they were done eating. They had to wait until the next day when God would give them more to eat. Some people complained again. They were very selfish. Some even took a bit of the manna flour and hid it until morning. In the morning the flour was full of worms and was rotten and smelled terrible. The people didn't listen to God and complained and whined instead.

God had a special day, the seventh day, called the Sabbath. He didn't want the people to work on the Sabbath so he told them that on the sixth day he wanted everyone to collect twice as much manna and use it for two days. Do you think that the manna got rotten overnight on the sixth night? No it didn't. God did another miracle and kept it fresh for two days. God was taking care of his people but they continued to complain. Some people do a lot of complaining.

How do you think it made everyone feel to hear the whining and complaining? How do you think it made God feel that the people were so selfish? Well the problem continued. Pretty soon they got

thirsty. Instead of asking God nicely for a drink they whined and complained some more. Can you believe it? They hadn't learned their lesson yet. Let's pretend that we are the Israelites who are thirsty and want a drink. What do you think their whining and complaining sounded like?

God told Moses to do another miracle to show the people that they didn't have to complain. All they had to do was trust God and he would provide for them. He told Moses to take his stick and hit it on a large rock. When he did, water started coming out of the rock and everyone had water to drink. God provided for them again. What would have been a better way to ask for water rather than whining or complaining? The Israelites had a lot to learn. It reminds me of children sometimes. Some kids whine and complain a lot. That's not honoring. In fact, it's selfish. God was trying to teach the Israelites how to ask nicely and it took them a long time to learn it. As we grow up, one of the things we learn is how not to whine and complain but how to solve problems in honoring ways. I want you to think about whining and complaining this week. Let's think of different ways to talk and get what we want besides whining and complaining. Then family life will be better and we will be doing what God wants us to do.

Our Bible verse this week gives us some good advice that the Israelites could have learned too.

Bible Verse:

Philippians 2:14 "Do everything without complaining or arguing."

Prayer:

Lord, thank you for providing so many things for us. Thank you for giving the Israelites a leader like Moses and thank you for giving our families leaders like our parents too. Please help us to learn how to solve problems without whining or complaining. Teach us what it means to be unselfish at home. Amen.

Session 3

Craft and Activity Time

15-20 minutes

Dough Art Frame

Supplies:

- Dough Art prepared ahead and place in plastic bags
- Photocopy the verse on card stock
- One foot square pieces of heavy cardboard (You may want to cut up several cardboard boxes)
- Fancy shaped noodles, buttons, and shells

Dough Art Recipe:

- 5 cups flour
- 2 1/2 cups salt
- 2 1/2 cups water
- Food coloring optional
- Mix dry ingredients in a bowl. Add coloring to the water, then mix in. Knead into a ball, adding more flour or water as needed. Store in a plastic bag until you use it. Be sure to make enough for the number of children you expect.

Instructions:

Prepare the dough ahead of time, following the recipe above. This recipe provides enough dough for 6-8 children, so double or triple the recipe as necessary. Divide the dough into balls 4" in diameter and place in individual plastic bags, one bag of dough for each child. Have children take the dough and press it out flat about 1/2 inch larger than the verse card. Press the verse card into the dough and then decorate the edge like a frame. You might use a fork to help create a design along the edges or allow the children to decorate with fancy shaped noodles, buttons, or shells. Allow children to leave their finished product on a piece of stiff cardboard. Write the child's name on the cardboard. You might keep them until the next session or allow the children to take them home. It will take several hours to dry hard. As an option, after they dry, you could shellac them to preserve them longer.

Activity
Role Play the "Wise Appeal"

The complete wise appeal is best taught to older children. Young kids can think of honoring ways to respond to the examples below. The wise appeal is used when a child isn't happy with a situation or a decision made by a parent. The child graciously appeals in a way that is gentle and non-threatening. Write the following formula on the board:

- I understand you want me to… because…
- I have a problem with that because…
- So could I please…

Now, give some common predicaments and ask children to create a wise appeal for that situation.

Example 1: You're watching TV and your mom says, "Son, your room is a mess. You need to go clean it up." How might you phrase a wise appeal in this situation? What would you do if your mom still says no?

Example 2: You come to your dad and ask him for permission to go over to a friend's house to play for the afternoon. Your dad says "no" because he's not sure that the things you're doing over there are all that good. How might you create a wise appeal? How might you respond if your dad says no? What are some other alternatives that might get a yes answer from Dad?

Example 3: Mom adds two more chores to your routine, taking out the trash and emptying the dishwasher. She also reduces your allowance. She says that you need to learn how to work hard and be more grateful for the things you have. How might you use a wise appeal in this situation? How might you respond if your Mom still says no?

Teacher Note:

When children argue, whine, or complain, parents often become more entrenched in their position. The wise appeal is a way for children to communicate with parents their concerns and offer alternative solutions. It's an honoring way to respond to problems.

Game

15-20 minutes

Balance the Ball Game

Have children divide into pairs. Give each pair a ball. You may want to provide different size balls from a tennis ball to a basketball. Give children the assignment to work together to hold the ball but to use only one finger each (or, if that's too hard, one finger from each hand) while they follow the directions you give them.

Ask them to walk to the other side of the room, go around a chair and return to their starting position. When multiple pairs of children try to do this at the same time, the job gets a little harder and requires more communication. The goal is to walk around the room without dropping the ball. You might also have the children reach down and touch a yellow square, then a green square, then a red square, touching pieces of construction paper arranged in the room.

Debrief with children about following directions. Sometimes obeying is hard because there are other things to consider. It's not easy to obey the instruction of the teacher when you have to hold a ball with someone else at the same time. Talk about how children feel when they fail, or when they are successful, or when they have to work with someone else to get a job done.

★ ★ ★ ★ ★

Snack

5-10 minutes

Wise Owl

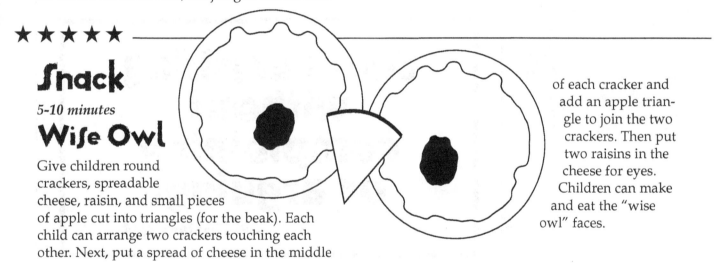

Give children round crackers, spreadable cheese, raisin, and small pieces of apple cut into triangles (for the beak). Each child can arrange two crackers touching each other. Next, put a spread of cheese in the middle of each cracker and add an apple triangle to join the two crackers. Then put two raisins in the cheese for eyes. Children can make and eat the "wise owl" faces.

★ ★ ★ ★ ★

Review and Close

5-10 minutes

Review the Three Finger Rule. Talk about why following instructions is important and how sometimes we need to **"Obey first and then we'll talk about it."** If your ball rolls into the street and you run after it. Your mom may call "stop" so you don't get hit by a car. You need to learn to obey Mom right away. That will keep you safe and teach you how to please God too.

With younger children you can role play the **"Come When You're Called Rule."** This rule emphasizes the importance of children responding to their parents right away. When a parent calls a child's name, that child should come to the parent and say, "What Mom" or "What Dad." Have children act out wrong responses when Mom calls and then have them act out the right response — to come the first time they are called. Review two choices the children have when Mom or Dad gives an instruction or a no answer. Instead of whining and complaining, choice one is to **Obey first and then we'll talk about it,** and choice two is the **Wise Appeal**.

Verse Card

Instructions:

Photocopy this page onto colored card stock. This page contains enough cards for three children. Cut on the dotted line. Gently push the card into the dough art and bring the dough over the edges of the card to keep it in place.

Sample of Dough Art Frame:

Do everything without complaining or arguing.

— Philippians 2:14

Do everything without complaining or arguing.

— Philippians 2:14

Do everything without complaining or arguing.

— Philippians 2:14

BE OBEY

- Do what someone says
- Right away
- Without being reminded

What Does Your Heart Look Like?

Preparing Your Heart to Teach Session 4:

There's a difference between going through the motions and experiencing a real heart change. Some people just focus on outward appearance, getting the right actions down. The result is an emphasis on image management. We all want more than that. Integrity is having our outward actions match our inner thoughts and attitudes.

The heart contains things like thoughts, motivations, fantasies, and desires. That's where the real work of growing in the Lord takes place. What kinds of things are you doing now in your life to contribute to significant heart change? Many people find encouragement to change their hearts through reading their Bibles, having a regular prayer time, or attending church for fellowship and service. In addition, you might memorize scripture, sacrifice for the benefit of others, or join some kind of accountability group.

Changing the heart isn't easy. Behavior change comes faster but real, lasting change takes place on a heart level. Proverbs 4:23 says, "Above all else, guard your heart, for it is the wellspring of life."

What is God working on in your life right now? Maybe it's anger, self-control, or patience. Are you just working on external behavior or are you looking for ways to make the deeper changes as well? Take a moment and think and pray about the heart issues that need adjustment. Sometimes it means releasing the desire to be in control or a demandingness about having things a certain way. Pray and ask God to help you change your heart in those areas.

What Children Learn in Session 4:

Children sometimes work hard to look good on the outside but their hearts just aren't changed. In fact, some children don't even realize how important the heart is so they simply change their behavior. In this session children will learn that God looks at the heart and that real change needs to take place on a deeper level. Using the story of Samuel looking for a king, children will realize the value of changing their hearts, not just their behavior.

A Summary of the Video Session 4:

Four goals are presented to help parents solve parenting problems. First, parents learn to be practical, helping their children know exactly what to do, not just what not to do. Second, the parents are challenged to work toward heart change in children, not just behavior change. Third, parents are encouraged to use the scriptures in day-to-day life with their children. Fourth, parents are encouraged to develop adult solutions to children's problems so that children can grow into mature responses that will strengthen them for the rest of their lives. *(parent training video series is optional)*

Read Along in the Book, "Say Goodbye to Whining, Complaining, and Bad Attitudes... In You and Your Kids":

Pages 13-23 talk about the importance of changing the heart. A diagram demonstrates a four-step approach parents can use as they develop heart-based discipline strategies.

Welcoming Activity

5-10 minutes

For Younger Children: Using the pattern given, have children decorate crowns. Sometimes a local hamburger restaurant will give you crowns to use. You can turn them inside out and decorate them.

For Older Children: Use the Seek and Find Puzzle sheet and ask children to find the character qualities in the puzzle.

★ ★ ★ ★ ★

Together Time

15-20 minutes

Use the thoughts and ideas below along with your own thoughts and the Bible to dialogue with the children and help them understand the importance of the heart.

Introduction:

Bring children together and talk about their crowns and how they decorated them. "If you saw someone with a crown what would you think about that person? Do you think that person would be a good person or a bad person?" (Don't answer this question but ask children for their feedback. The answer will come later in the lesson. The point is that many people make judgments about a person based on appearance when there's much more under the surface that determines a person's character.) For older children, you can talk about which words were the hardest to find in the puzzle and which ones are the hardest to live out.

Object Lesson:

Bring two wrapped gifts, one messily wrapped in newspaper and the other bigger and neatly wrapped in pretty wrapping paper. Ask the children which one they wish they could have? Why? Talk about what might be inside each of them and how you can't tell what's inside by just looking at the outside. Don't open the gifts until the

story is over. Then open them both to reveal shredded newspaper in the big, nicely wrapped box and stickers for each child in the small, poorly wrapped box. For older children you may want to substitute wrapped candy for stickers.

Bible Story with Application:

Read the story for yourself in 1 Samuel 16:1-13 and then use the ideas you learn plus the ideas that follow to tell children the Bible story, teaching them the importance of the heart, not just behavior.

God had a job for Samuel the prophet. It was time to get a new king and it was Samuel's job to anoint him. God didn't tell Samuel who the king was but only told him which family to look for. So Samuel started off toward Bethlehem to find the family of Jesse. I wonder what he thought as he was walking along. Samuel had liked the first king quite a bit. His name was Saul. He was tall and handsome and the people liked him but he wasn't very good at following directions.

Sometimes when God gave Saul a job to do, Saul didn't obey. He would just do whatever he wanted to do. He didn't know how to follow instructions. That means that he wasn't a very good leader so God decided to replace him as king. Now it was Samuel's job to find someone else. Who would it be this time?

When Samuel came to the town where Jesse lived, God told him to offer a sacrifice and invite Jesse's family to attend the special meal together with him. This would be the way that Samuel would get to meet the boys and then he would know which one would be the next king. Jesse introduced each one of his sons to Samuel who wondered, "Is this the one that God wants to be king?"

The first boy to come was Eliab. He was the oldest and Samuel just knew he must be the one. After all he looked good and he was tall. He looked like the kind of person who could be a king. But God already tried a person who looked good — Saul — and he didn't make a very good king. So God told Samuel a very important thing. Part of what God said is actually our Bible verse

for today. "Do not consider his appearance or his height, for I have rejected him. The Lord does not look at the things man looks at. Man looks at the outward appearance, but the Lord looks at the heart."

"Mmmm. God looks at the heart," thought Samuel. "I wonder who it will be? How will I know which one should be the next king? I can't see into a person's heart."

The next son to come by was Abinadab and then another and another, seven in all. Each time he met a new son, Samuel knew that he just wasn't the right one to be king. God was looking for someone very special to lead the nation. He wanted someone who had the right heart. Samuel came to the end of the line up. No one was left. Samuel said to Jesse, "Are these all the sons you have?"

Jesse did have one other son but he was just a kid. He was out taking care of the sheep. "There's still the youngest," he said.

"Send for him," Samuel said. So they waited. Samuel wouldn't sit down to eat without knowing who it was that God wanted to be king. Then the last boy came. He was young but God told Samuel that he was the right one. His name was David. He had the right heart. God knew that David would listen to him and follow directions. That's why God gave David the most important

job in the whole nation. God chose David to be king.

God has an important job for each of you. You may not know what that job is yet but God does. The most important thing you can do right now to get ready for the job is to have the right kind of heart. God knows what's in your heart. He knows when you try to follow directions, show kindness to others, and want to do the right thing.

Let's look at our two presents again. Which one of them should we open first? Open the big, nicely wrapped one (with the shredded newspaper inside). Hmmm. Not such a nice present is it? It looked good on the outside but when you opened it up, it wasn't so good. Let's open the smaller one. Distribute the stickers (or candy) to the children. It's not so much what it looks like on the outside but what's on the inside that counts.

Bible Verse:

1 Samuel 16:7 "The LORD does not look at the things man looks at. Man looks at the outward appearance, but the LORD looks at the heart."

Prayer:

Lord, show us the things in our hearts that need to change. Help us to love you with all of our hearts and teach us how to follow directions and do what's right. We love you and want to serve you. Amen.

Session 4

Craft and Activity Time

15-20 minutes

Character Quality People

Supplies Needed:

- 9 brads per student
- Photocopy the activity sheet for each student

Instructions:

For Younger Children: Cut out the parts and assemble the people in advance. Allow the children to color the body parts with crayons or markers.

For Older Children: Allow each child to cut out the body parts and assemble the people with brads. Talk about the various character qualities, and which ones the children think are most important.

★ ★ ★ ★ ★

Game

15-20 minutes

Fruit Basket Upset

Have children sit in a circle. Assign names of the fruit of the Spirit—love, joy, peace, patience, kindness, goodness, faithfulness, gentleness, and self control—to each child making sure that you choose only as many "fruits" as needed to have three or four children per fruit. Have one child stand in the center of the circle leaving no empty places in the circle. The leader calls out one fruit name, "joy." All the children who were assigned joy must get up and find another seat and the person in the center takes one of their seats. This will leave a new child in the center. Call a different fruit and continue the game. You may also choose two fruits at the same time or call "All the fruit" which means everyone must find a different seat. It's best to have tape or mats on the floor to identify available spaces otherwise everyone will find a place.

Activity
Treasure Hunt

In advance glue pictures from magazines onto construction paper. For young children use different color construction paper so that each puzzle is a unique color. Turn the pictures over and write the location of a treat on the back. Cut the pictures into four parts. Make as many of these puzzles as needed so that each child in the class gets one piece of one puzzle. Mix up all the puzzle pieces in a bag and allow each child to choose one. Any extra pieces should be displayed in the front of the room for the children to take if they are needed for their puzzle. Tell children to find other children with matching pieces and to form a group. When their puzzle is complete they should turn it over to reveal the location of a treat.

Talk about how the real treasures in life come when people develop character and have hearts that are doing the right thing. Take time to review the Bible verse.

Snack

5-10 minutes

Character Quality Fruit Salad

Bring containers of cut fruit. Make a fruit salad as you talk about the different fruit of the Spirit. You can either allow children to make the salad themselves or you can just make one big salad and then serve it to all.

Review and Close:

5-10 minutes

How can you grow in patience, kindness, or peace? Spend time talking about how a child can grow in one of these areas. Children often have interesting ideas about how character develops. You might share some personal experiences of things that have happened in your life to develop a particular character quality.

Seek and Find Puzzle
Fruit of the Spirit

Instructions:

Find the words in the boxes below. They can go in any direction: horizontal, vertical, or diagonal; forward, or backward. Draw a circle around each word.

LOVE	PATIENCE	FAITHFULNESS
JOY	KINDNESS	GENTLENESS
PEACE	GOODNESS	SELF CONTROL

S	Z	X	C	V	B	N	M	A	S	D	F	G	H	J
U	E	L	O	V	E	L	Q	W	E	R	T	Y	U	K
S	I	L	O	P	Z	X	C	V	B	N	K	M	A	P
S	S	G	F	D	F	G	H	J	K	I	P	L	Q	A
E	Q	O	W	C	J	E	R	T	N	Y	E	U	I	T
N	I	O	O	P	O	Z	X	D	C	V	A	B	N	I
E	N	D	M	A	Y	N	N	S	D	F	C	G	H	E
L	H	N	J	K	L	E	T	Q	W	E	E	R	T	N
T	Y	E	U	I	S	O	P	R	Z	X	C	V	B	C
N	N	S	M	S	A	S	D	F	O	G	H	J	K	E
E	L	S	Q	W	E	R	T	Y	U	L	I	O	P	Z
G	C	F	A	I	T	H	F	U	L	N	E	S	S	X

Character Quality People

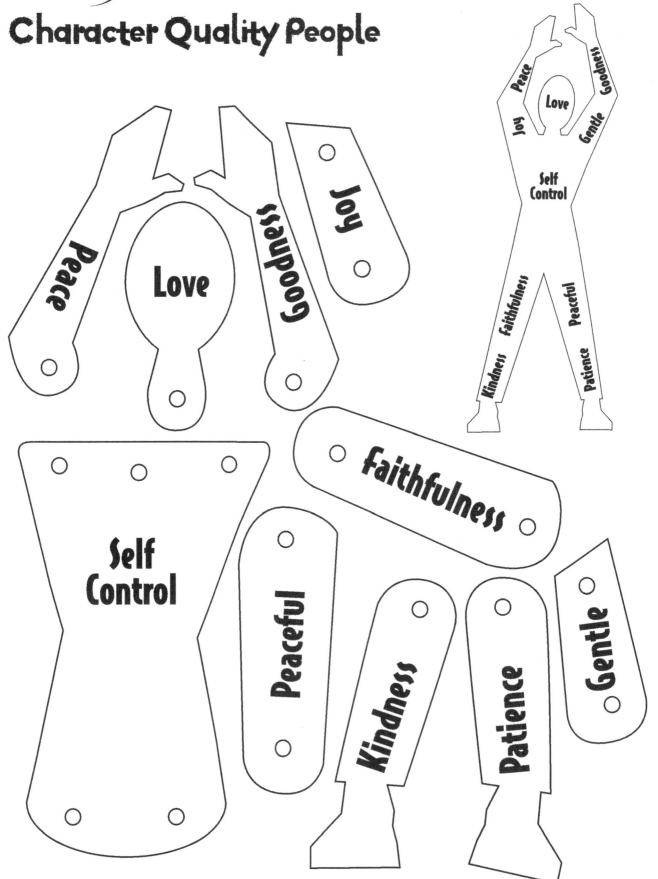

Crown Template for Welcoming Activity

Instructions: Photocopy crown onto construction paper. Use a 2" strip of construction paper to adjust to fit child's head.

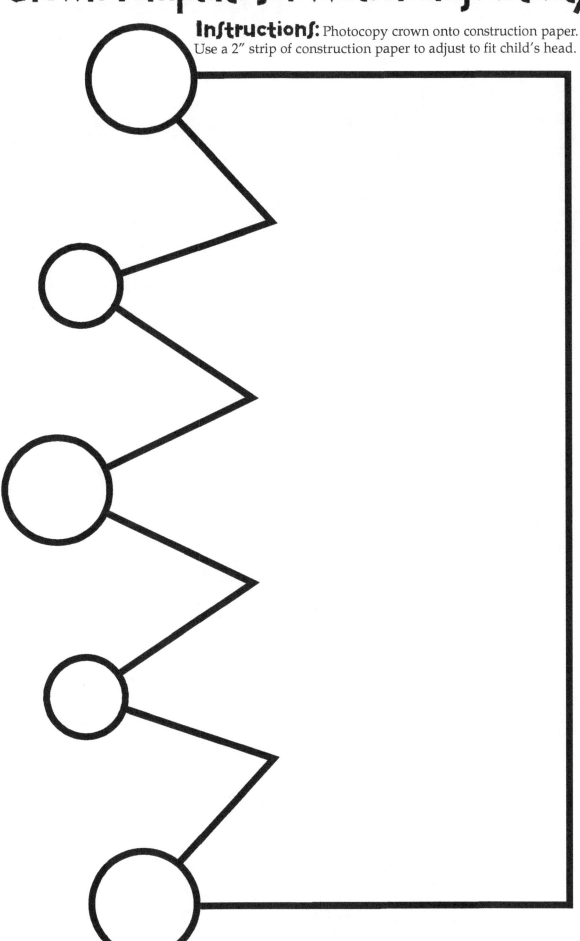

It's All In How You Say It

Preparing Your Heart to Teach Session 5:

As a teacher, how do you handle children who are not following directions, becoming wild, or who have to be reminded several times to do something? The temptation may be to become harsh, but harshness has some negative side effects that add more friction to a relationship. A better solution is to be firm without being harsh.

Firmness is establishing a boundary that can't be crossed without experiencing a consequence. Harshness pours emotional intensity into the situation to try to convince the person that you mean business. Usually people become harsh because they don't have a plan for firmness. James 1:20 says it well, "Anger does not bring about the righteous life that God desires."

Do you resort to harshness to get things done? What kinds of things tend to move you into a harshness mode? Consider some different strategies that apply firmness without harshness. It might mean getting closer to the child and obtaining his or her full attention before giving an instruction, reinforcing what you've asked, or following through more quickly with a consequence.

In the end your ability to be firm without being harsh will help children know that you mean business and will preserve relationships in the process.

What Children Learn in Session 5:

Often children don't realize the significance of their words. Many kids just say whatever comes to their minds. In this lesson children will learn how important their words are and that the way they say their words communicates something as

well. The story of Mordecai and Haman will reveal the dangers of using words to boast. Activities and the craft will bring out the idea that words can hurt or help people in ways we don't even realize.

A Summary of the Video Session 5:

Honor is a two-way street. Children need to honor their parents, but parents also need to learn to honor their children. Parents often fall into extremes in parenting. Either they become too lenient, wanting to please their children, or they become too strict and overly controlling. Honor-based parenting requires a number of skills, and since many parents don't have a good history with honor in their own family growing up, these skills provide a helpful framework. This session focuses on one skill, "Being firm without being harsh." Parents learn that firmness sets a boundary that won't be crossed without a consequence, and that harshness pours emotional intensity into that limit to try to convince a child that you mean business. Suggestions are given for handling bedtimes. With a tighter action point and clearer consequences, parents can replace their harshness with honor.
(parent training video series is optional)

Read Along in the Book, "Say Goodbye to Whining, Complaining, and Bad Attitudes... In You and Your Kids":

Pages 89-106 teach parents ways to communicate without anger. Children also need to learn good communication skills so that their words will help bring about positive change rather than just be hurtful.

Welcoming Activity

5-10 minutes

Use the photocopied frame to draw a picture of your family. Because the term "family" may be different for each child, you may want to say something like, "Draw a picture of all the people that live in your house." If children live in more than one house it may be best to draw a line in the frame and have the child draw two pictures.

For Older Children: Many older children will enjoy the above project but another welcome activity is available if needed. Have children do the Seek and Find Puzzle, hunting for a number of key words from today's lesson.

Together Time

15-20 minutes

Use the thoughts and ideas below along with your own thoughts and the Bible to dialogue with the children and help them understand the importance of honoring others with their words.

Introduction:

Let's see your picture of your family. Which one are you in the picture? How many of you have three people, four people, five people, etc. in your family? All families are different aren't they? In fact, some people come into a family through adoption, some are born right into that family and others come in when two parents who already have children get married. Families are like a laboratory and are a place where we can learn and grow so that we can be successful with others in life.

Object Lesson:
Pepper Illustration

Be prepared with the following supplies: a dinner plate, a large glass of water, a shaker of black pepper, and a small amount of dish soap in a bowl (the secret ingredient). Have children close enough to observe what happens. You may need to do this with small groups if you have a large number of children.

Fill the plate with water almost to its edge and talk about how the water in the plate represents relationships. Then say, "Some people only think about themselves. They boast about how good they are. Do you like to spend time with that kind of person? When that happens, people aren't happy, and others aren't happy with them." Boasting and pride are like this ingredient here. (Sprinkle a good amount of pepper onto the water.) It makes relationships dirty and unpleasant like this pepper does to our water.

"I have a secret ingredient that's going to do something to all that pepper." Now dip your finger into the bowl of soap and then touch it into the water on the edge of the dish. All the pepper will move to the opposite side. "Today I want to tell you about a secret ingredient in life that works just like that in your family to deal with a lot of the negative words in family life. That secret ingredient is honor and as members of the Honor Club we're going to learn more about it today.

Bible Story with Application:

Read Esther 5:11-6:12 and use the ideas you learn and some of these thoughts to tell the Bible story.

Haman was a prideful man. He wanted everyone to notice him. If something was going on, he wanted to be right at the center of it. When Haman drove by in his chariot he wanted everyone to bow down low to show respect for him. He said to his wife, "I am rich and have so much money. The king thinks I am very important. The queen only invited two people to her house for dinner, the king and me. I am a very important person."

But Haman had a problem. There was a man in the town who loved the Lord and who wouldn't bow down to Haman. His name was Mordecai. This made Haman very angry. In fact,

Haman couldn't enjoy all the good things that he had because he was angry in his heart toward Mordecai. Every day he would get mad and he wished that he could find a way to get rid of this guy who wouldn't bow down to him.

One day Haman went to work and the king called for him. "Haman, I have someone I want to honor. I need an idea of how to show how valuable this man is to me."

Haman thought, "Oh, the king must be talking about me. I'm so important to the king. He must want to tell everyone in the kingdom how great I am." So, Haman told the king his idea. "I think you should put him on one of your horses and let him wear one of your robes and put a crown on his head and let someone else lead this man around town and announce to everyone that this person is special to the king."

As Haman imagined himself on that horse, wearing the king's robe, and a crown on his head, the king said, "Good idea, Haman. I'd like you to be the one to lead the horse."

"What?" thought Haman in shock as he continued to listen to the king.

"Yes, I want you to do all those nice things to Mordecai."

Haman couldn't believe his ears. He had boasted and been so proud and been so angry with Mordecai every day. This was the worst thing he could ever imagine happening. Now he had to give honor to Mordecai. It was terrible.

That's a true story and it illustrates something very important about honor. Some people try to build themselves up by boasting and talking about how good they are. Those people are always in danger. Someday something will happen that will humble them.

People who understand honor don't boast about themselves. They look for ways to build others up. Our mouths can get us into a lot of trouble sometimes. Members of the Honor Club look for ways to care for others and not just focus on ourselves. Our Bible verse talks about pride.

Bible Verse:

Proverbs 18:12 "Before his downfall a man's heart is proud, but humility comes before honor."

Prayer:

Lord, teach us how to honor others instead of just building ourselves up. Help us to think of ways to make others feel special. Thank you for loving us and treating us as special. Amen.

Craft and Activity Time

15-20 minutes

Door Knob Sign

Supplies Needed:

- Photocopy the activity sheet onto card stock
- Markers

Discussion:

As children decorate the Door Knob Signs, talk to them about honoring and dishonoring words in family life.

Activity

Color the picture of the heart and the trash can beforehand and put them on the wall. Cut out the strips of paper with honoring and dishonoring words on them. Hand out the strips of paper and have a child read the strip with expression and then tape it on the Heart or the Trash Can depending on whether it is honoring or dishonoring. You may want to make more blank strips and add your own phrases or have children help you think of more. For younger children you'll want to read them all and then have the children tape them up.

After completing all the prepared statements, brainstorm with the kids for other ideas of dishonoring and honoring kinds of speech, write them on strips of paper and have the children tape them up.

★ ★ ★ ★ ★

Game

15-20 minutes

Honor Bingo

Instructions:

Use the enclosed template to make a Bingo card for each child. Have each child color eight pictures and then glue them onto the Bingo card in any order they'd like. As the teacher, you also color all the pictures but don't put them on the card. Your pictures will be chosen at random to show children so they can mark their cards.

Bring beans or pieces of paper to place in the appropriate squares. Hold up one little picture at a time and ask, "What's happening in this picture?" Children identify the picture and then make a comment about obedience or honor; then continue with the Bingo game. Play the game several times asking children to get three in a row, or the four corners, or the whole card.

Take this opportunity to review the Bible verse and talk about pride and humility in family life.

★ ★ ★ ★ ★

Snack

5-10 minutes

Using a cereal or other food that's shaped like letters allow children to spell out the words used in the Seek and Find Puzzle. For younger children,

you may want to put the letters on the board for the word honor. Help children identify each letter, find them among the cereal, and then enjoy eating them. Talk about honoring and dishonoring things family members say.

Review and Close

5-10 minutes

Read the following story to the children and then discuss it together. Talk about the value of our words as we communicate with each other.

A Story About Words

"Hi, Karen," said Grandma as they passed each other by the mailbox. Grandma and Grandpa lived on the same property as their son and his family. Karen was 13 years old and enjoyed spending time with Grandma. "I talked to your parents about us going up to RJ's for hamburgers for dinner tonight," Grandma continued.

"Oh, no," said Karen. "We can't go there."

"Why not?" asked Grandma puzzled. "RJ's has always been your favorite place for hamburgers. You usually beg us to take you there."

"Yeah, that was until I found out how they make those hamburgers."

"What do you mean?" Grandma asked.

"Those hamburgers are so juicy because they put worms in with the meat when they cook them."

"Oh, that's silly," said Grandma, "Where did you ever hear something like that?"

"Everyone knows that, " continued Karen. "All my friends have heard about it."

"That's ridiculous," shuttered Grandma. "First of all, it would be illegal."

"Well they just sneak them in and no one knows about it."

"Karen, that's just a rumor and you better be careful about believing everything you hear. Let me tell you a story about rumors."

Grandma and Karen sat down on the porch as Grandma continued.

I read in the paper yesterday that two boys, James and Philip, were playing with matches. They are only 10 years old but they thought that matches were pretty fun and took some out to the field where no one could see what they were doing. Matches make fires and a fire can be a good thing in a fireplace or in a grill for cooking but these boys were just playing around and didn't realize what trouble they would cause. They were lighting the matches and throwing them around. It was a very foolish thing to do. Do you know what happened?

Some of the grass started to catch fire. The boys watched it for a moment because it looked pretty interesting to them and besides, they could stamp it out with their feet, it was so small. But the wind came up and the fire started to spread quickly. They tried to put it out but it just continued to grow. Pretty soon the fire was so big that they couldn't do anything about it. It was burning the whole field.

Philip and James ran back to James' house and his mom called the fire department. The firemen came and tried to contain the fire but it spread to a forest area and ended up burning part of one house. It was a very sad story and Philip and James are now in a lot of trouble.

"That's an interesting story," said Karen, "but what does that have to do with worms in the hamburgers?"

Ask the children, "Do any of you children know how those two stories are related? What do worms in hamburgers have to do with the fire caused by James and Philip?" Let's listen some more.

Grandma said, "Let me tell you how these two stories relate. Rumors are like fire. They start small but pretty soon they get out of control and they do a lot of damage. How many people don't want to go to RJ's now because of this rumor? How much business have they lost? You see, we need to be very careful about the things we say. James 3:5 tells us that our tongue is like a fire. It can cause a lot of damage if we aren't careful. Rumors are just one way. Boasting, whining and complaining, and lying are other ways that our tongue can hurt other people."

You wouldn't play with matches would you? No. That would not be good. But what about your tongue? Maybe your tongue is doing more damage than you think. The best thing we can do is ask ourselves the question "Is what I'm going to say helpful or not." That will help us know if we're doing the right thing with our mouths.

What's something honoring that you might try to say this week in your family? Let several children answer and then brainstorm of other ways children might be honoring with their words.

Welcoming Activity Frame for Family Picture

Door Knob Sign

Instructions: Photocopy onto card stock. This page contains enough signs for two children. Allow child to cut and color.

Seek and Find Puzzle
It's All in How You Say It

Instructions:

Find the words in the boxes below. They can go in any direction: horizontal, vertical, or diagonal; forward, or backward. Draw a circle around each word.

HUMILITY	HONOR	HARSH
PRIDE	ENCOURAGE	WHINING
LYING	COMPLAINING	BOASTING
FIRMNESS	FORGIVENESS	

E	Z	X	C	V	H	U	M	I	L	I	T	Y	B	P
N	N	M	A	S	O	D	F	G	H	J	K	L	R	Q
W	E	C	R	T	N	Y	U	I	O	P	Z	I	X	C
V	B	N	O	M	O	A	S	D	F	G	D	H	J	K
R	Q	W	E	U	R	T	Y	U	I	E	O	W	P	G
L	Z	X	C	V	R	B	N	M	A	S	D	W	F	N
L	G	H	J	K	L	A	Q	W	E	R	T	H	Y	I
Y	U	I	O	P	Z	X	G	C	V	B	N	I	M	T
I	A	S	F	I	R	M	N	E	S	S	D	N	F	S
N	S	S	E	N	E	V	I	G	R	O	F	I	E	A
G	Q	W	C	O	M	P	L	A	I	N	I	N	G	O
R	T	Y	H	A	R	S	H	U	I	O	P	G	Z	B

Honoring Words Activity

Instructions: Cut out and color for Session 5 class activity.

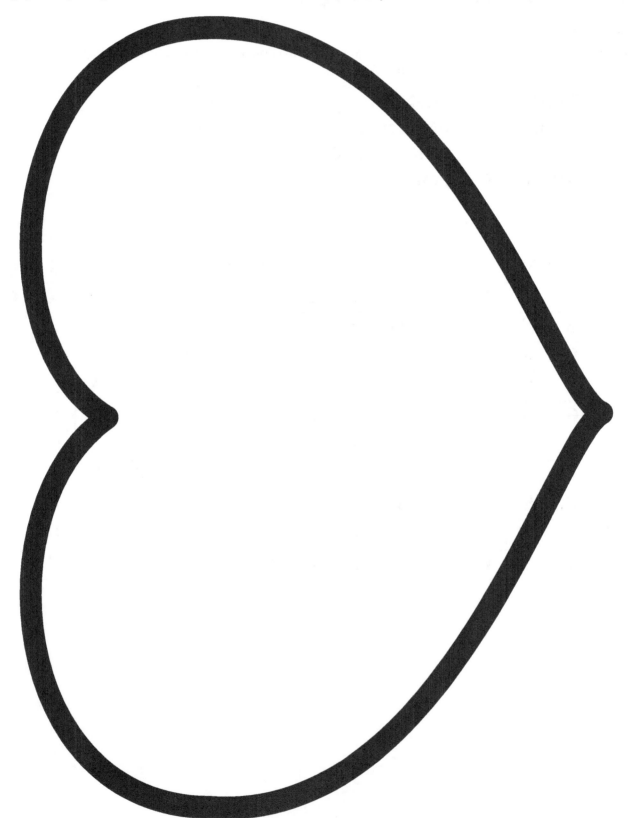

Honoring Words Activity

Instructions:

Cut out and color for
Session 5 class activity.

Honoring Words Activity

Instructions: Cut out for Session 5 class activity.

That shirt looks nice.

My story is the best!

Thank you.

Are we there yet?

Would you like a piece of my candy?

Hey, Gimme my tape now!

I like the way you drew that picture.

No you can't have any.

They're all mine.

I'm sorry for hurting your feelings.

Oh yuck, I hate that dinner.

I think it's your turn to go first.

Honor Bingo • Bingo Card Template

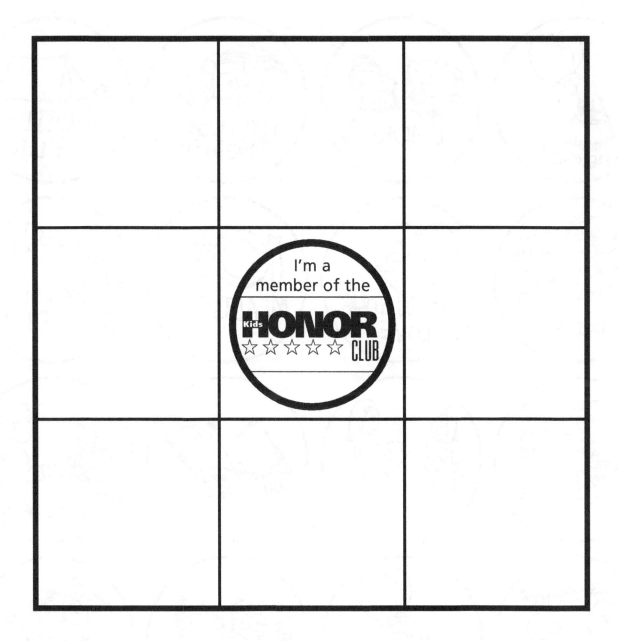

Honor Bingo · Pictures for the Bingo Cards

Problems Contain Hidden Opportunities

Preparing Your Heart to Teach Session 6:

Problems are opportunities, at least that seems to be the way Jesus viewed them. Many times Jesus used the common problems his followers faced to teach them some new aspect of God's character or about wisdom in life. When the crowds were hungry in Matthew 14:16, Jesus said to his disciples, "You give them something to eat." In Mark 4:38-39 the lake was stormy the disciples woke up Jesus with a problem, "Teacher, don't you care if we drown?" He got up, rebuked the wind and said to the waves, "Quiet! Be still!" Then the wind died down and it was completely calm. When the disciples couldn't cast a demon out of the boy in Mark 9:28-29 they brought the problem to Jesus who used the opportunity to teach about prayer. It seems that Jesus was able to find a teaching opportunity in every problem his disciples experienced.

As you work with children do you view problems as irritations to get rid of or as opportunities for teaching? It's interesting that sometimes parents get frustrated because they feel their children aren't motivated to learn. Problems are one of the great motivators of life. If we solve a problem too quickly for a child then we sometimes lose the teaching opportunity.

Just think about your own life. What problems have you encountered, big or small, that challenged you to learn some new things? It's amazing how often it happens. Construction on the road forces you to learn a new and better route to work. Sickness gives you greater empathy for others who are ill. Conflict in a relationship forces you to talk about issues that are unpleasant.

The next time a child brings you a problem, take an extra moment and ask yourself how you might use the situation as an opportunity to teach

something about life. It's amazing how character qualities like perseverance and faith, can be taught through the every day problems of life.

What Children Learn in Session 6:

Some people view problems as intrusions into their lives and respond with anger or a bad attitude. This session will introduce problems to children as opportunities to grow, learn, and develop problem-solving skills they'll need to be successful. Instead of expecting parents and others to solve problems for them, children will learn that solving their own problems is a sign of their maturity. The Bible story of Jesus working with his disciples to feed 5,000 people illustrates the way Jesus used a problem to teach the disciples an important lesson.

A Summary of the Video Session 6:

Three more honor-based parenting skills are presented in this session. "Use sorrow instead of anger in the discipline process" reflects the way God grieves when we sin against him as mentioned in Ephesians 4:30. "Use decision-making and problem-solving to teach honor" helps parents know when to step in and how to use common everyday experiences in the teaching process. And "Envision a positive future" helps parents to focus on the positive qualities in their children so they can encourage their kids with a preview of a successful future. Jesus is used as a model of balance as he worked with his disciples. *(parent training video series is optional)*

Read Along in the Book,
"Say Goodbye to Whining, Complaining, and Bad Attitudes... In You and Your Kids":

Pages 106-109 suggest the value of using problems to teach children honor. Instead of just solving the problem with kids, why not use the opportunity presented to teach children how we solve them.

★ ★ ★ ★ ★

Welcoming Activity

5-10 minutes

As children arrive, direct them to a table where they can begin decorating their sunglasses. The craft time will continue this activity later but it is a fun way to get children involved right away as they enter the room.

★ ★ ★ ★ ★

Together Time

15-20 minutes

Use the thoughts and ideas below along with your own thoughts and the Bible to dialogue with the children about how members of the Honor Club look for ways to solve problems and help others.

Introduction:

Have children model their glasses. If you have a Polaroid camera, you may want to take a picture of the children and allow them to watch it develop. If not, a film or digital camera will allow children to see themselves at a later time. Tell children that when we're in the Honor Club we see things differently. We look for ways to honor others.

Object Lesson:

Help children understand that there are often many sides to a situation, and that we can't always know the whole story. Give each child a sheet of scrap paper. Have each student poke a hole in the center of the paper with a pencil. Then have the children hold their papers up and look through the holes. Ask them what they can see. Next, have them put their papers down and look in the same direction. Has the scene change? What do they see now? What is the difference between what they saw through the hole and what they see without it?

Bible Story with Application:

Read Matthew 14:13-21. Use the ideas you get from the story and the following thoughts to tell the Bible story emphasizing the way that Jesus let his disciples solve the problem themselves.

Jesus had just heard that his friend, John the Baptist, was killed. He was sad and wanted to be alone so he went out to the country where he could have some quiet time. When people heard that Jesus was alone, they came to find him so that they could be healed. Jesus took time to help them.

Do you ever feel like you just want to be alone? Where do you go for some quiet time? Let the kids share and then share yourself about a place you like to be alone.

After working with people for most of the day, it started to get dark. The disciples thought about the people getting hungry and so they came to Jesus with the problem. The disciples liked to

bring problems to Jesus. Sometimes Jesus would go ahead and solve the problem and other times he would give them ideas for solving the problem themselves. This time he just gave the problem back on them to try to solve it themselves. He said, "You give them something to eat."

Why do you think Jesus did that? Do you think Jesus could have solved this problem by himself? Then why did he tell the disciples to solve it? He knew the disciples didn't have any food. I think Jesus wanted to teach them how to solve problems for themselves. I wonder if there are some times in your family when your mom or your dad encourage you to solve your own problem. Can you think of a time that they told you to solve a problem yourself instead of solving it for you? Maybe you lost your shoes and they told you to go find them. Maybe you wanted a drink and they encouraged you to get one yourself. Maybe you wanted to buy something special and your parents made you earn the money for it. Why do moms and dads do that? Why don't they just solve the problem for you?

Sometimes the loving thing is for a parent not to solve a problem so that you can learn to solve problems for yourself. Sometimes kids can get lazy and rely too much on others to solve their problems. Jesus wanted to teach the disciples

how to solve problems for themselves and how to trust God in that process.

The disciples looked at each other and then started looking for food. Somehow they found a small boy who had a lunch of five small rolls and two fish. They brought the food to Jesus and he did a miracle. The Bible tells us that he prayed and then began breaking the bread and the fish. Then the food just kept coming and coming. Pretty soon there was enough food for all the people to have plenty and there was even some left over.

How do you think the disciples felt as they watched all of that happen? What do you think they learned that day? Sometimes we learn things by solving the problem ourselves. Our Bible verse today reminds us to be confident even when we find ourselves with tough problems.

Bible Verse:

Philippians 4:13 "I can do everything through him who gives me strength."

Prayer:

Lord, thank you for helping us solve problems. Help us to view problems as opportunities instead of interruptions to our lives. Teach us to rely on you more. Amen.

★ ★ ★ ★ ★

Craft and Activity Time

15-20 minutes

Funny Glasses and Listening Ears

Supplies Needed:

- Photocopy the glasses and ears for each child
- Two rubber bands per child
- A single hole punch
- Chenille wire (pipe cleaners)

Instructions:

After decorating them with markers or crayons, have each child cut out two ears and the glasses and then punch a hole where indicated. For younger children, you will want to cut out the lens part of the eyeglasses ahead of time. Loop a rubber band through the hole in the ears and then pull the other end through the loop to attach the rubber band to the paper ears. The rubber band can then go around the child's ears. Put chenille wire through the hole in the glasses and mold it around the child's ear to hold them on like glasses.

Discussion:

Children in the Honor Club see problems as opportunities. It's like they have special glasses and special ears to listen and see things differently. We look for solutions instead of just complaining. We look to work together to solve problems because we know that *how* we solve a problem is just as important as solving it.

Talk about the Bible verse again and how Jesus can help us do more than we thought we could.

Activity

Divide children into groups of four or five. Give each child in a group a different color marker. Give each group a large piece of poster board and an assignment to draw a picture using all the colors. You may tell them what to draw, i.e. a house, or let them decide. Each child must participate in the picture though and use only his or her own color. All colors must be represented in the picture. Discuss the benefits of working together as a team to solve the problem and come up with a beautiful picture.

★ ★ ★ ★ ★

Game

15-20 minutes

Ping Pong Ball Balance Game

Have several ping pong balls and pieces of poster board available, one for each group of four children. Ask children to work together, one holding each corner or side of the poster board and do the following tasks:

- Just keep the ball in the center of the poster board.
- Lower the poster board to the ground without dropping the ball.
- Make the ball roll in a circle clockwise and then counterclockwise.

As children are doing these tasks ask them to look for ways to be encouraging as they give instructions to others, offer words of correction, or if the ball falls off the cardboard. Talk about positive things to say that add energy to the game. Also, talk about negative things people can say that focus on the problem instead of the solution. Talk about how different comments make people feel.

Snack

5-10 minutes

In keeping with the Bible story, purchase oyster crackers and little crackers shaped like fish. Of course these are different than the food that was served to the crowd, but it's a fun way to tie in the Bible story and remind children of the details.

Review and Close

5-10 minutes

Use the following case studies to help the students develop solutions for the children in the stories. Talk about solving problems and help children explore different solutions than they're used to.

- Bill lost his shoe. It wasn't under the bed with his other one. What are some ways Bill could solve this problem besides getting upset?

You might suggest that Bill look again, look other places in his room, stop and think about the last place he had his shoes, and ask Dad or Mom nicely for help.

- Sarah's friend Mindy wants to play with her and wants Sarah to exclude Kayla. Sarah would like to play with both Mindy and Kayla. How might Sarah handle this problem?

You might suggest that Sarah talk about it more with Mindy and maybe set up some time to just play with Mindy alone and other times to include Kayla. You may suggest that Sarah should take a stand for righteousness at this point and just tell Mindy that she won't exclude Kayla. How might you do this graciously?

- Tom's mom said "no" when he asked her if he could go over to a friend's house and play for the afternoon. How might Tom handle this problem without becoming mean to Mom?

Handling disappointment is a challenge for every child. You might explore the idea of Tom appealing to Mom or trying to understand why Mom is saying "no." Tom should avoid whining, badgering, or complaining and may need to accept the "no" answer and say to himself, "maybe next time."

Instructions:

Color the ears and the glasses and then cut them out carefully on the line. Punch holes in the place where indicated. Loop a rubber band through the hole in the ear and then bring that loop through the loop in the other end of the rubber band and pull tight but don't rip the paper. Put the rubber band around the ear. Use chenille wire to create ear pieces for the glasses and run them through the holes where indicated.

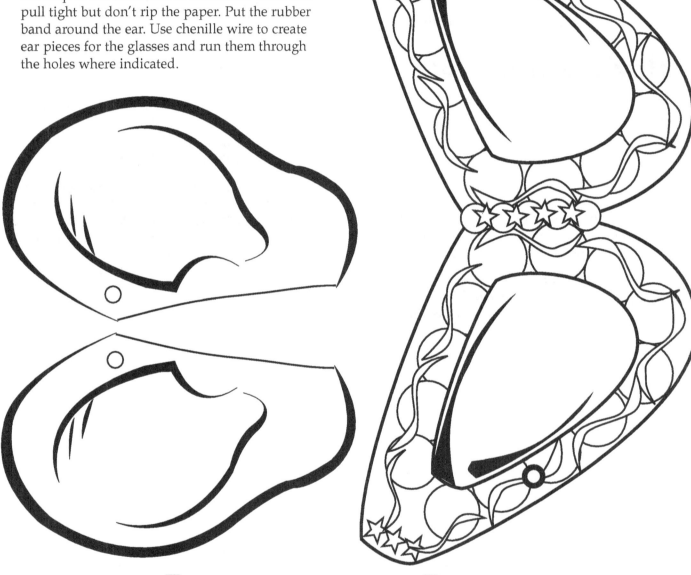

Look for Solutions Not Problems

Reserving a Little to Give Away

Preparing Your Heart to Teach Session 7:

A margin is an extra amount set aside for contingencies or emergencies. Everyday life needs a little margin of time for the unexpected. But those who don't plan margins into their schedule usually don't have them. Life can get very complicated very quickly and only those who are intentional have a little of themselves left over when the pressures of life increase.

Usually honoring others requires extra time or energy. Many people live so close to the edge that they don't have anything left to give for an unexpected act of kindness. In the story of the Good Samaritan in Luke 10:30-36, one man, although not as religious as the others, had enough margin in his life that he could help someone in need. Jesus commended him by asking the disciples, "Which of these three do you think was a neighbor to the man who fell into the hands of robbers?" The obvious answer was the man who had time and took initiative to give of himself.

It's the small things that often count the most. The smile or kind word, an encouraging observation or compliment can brighten a person's day. Take a few moments and reflect on your own life. Is it so crowded with activities and things to do that you can't show honor to others? If you don't have time for an unexpected act of kindness every once in a while, then maybe you need to reevaluate your life. Being available to give small gifts of kindness will bring joy into your life as well as the lives of others.

What Children Learn in Session 7:

Honor is something to give to others. Using the story of the Good Samaritan children will explore ways that they can share honor outside their families as well as inside. Sometimes children become self-focused and need some help thinking about others. This session prompts them to do just that.

A Summary of the Video Session 7:

Can you honor your family too much? Yes, we believe you can. A family can become so inwardly focused that it encourages selfishness. The solution is to work as a family to give honor away. Then children see that their family has a special gift that they can pass on to others. A family actually grows closer together as they learn to reach out with honor. Practical ideas are shared of how a family can show honor to others.
(parent training video series is optional)

Read Along in the Book, "Say Goodbye to Whining, Complaining, and Bad Attitudes... In You and Your Kids":

Pages 165-178 address the question, "Can you honor your family too much?" The point of this chapter is that your family actually grows in honor as you work as a team to give it away.

Welcoming Activity

5-10 minutes

As children arrive have them decorate cookies with icing. You may purchase these cookies at the store or bake them yourself. Bring icing and various sprinkles or decorations to put on them. Tell the children they can each decorate two cookies, one to give away and one to eat a little later in the session. Provide plastic bags or wrap to protect the cookies that the children will take home and give away.

Together Time

15-20 minutes

Use the thoughts and ideas below along with your own thoughts and the Bible to help children understand that honor is something that we give away.

Introduction:

Talk to children about their cookies. What was their favorite sprinkle? Who are they going to give the extra cookie to?

Object Lesson:

Bring several small objects that could be used to help accomplish a task and put those objects in a bag that you keep hidden. One at a time, place the objects in a large sock and allow a child to reach in and feel what the object is. They shouldn't tell anyone what they feel or what the object is. Instead, the child should tell everyone how this object might be used to help. Other
children try to guess what's in the sock. The one who guesses gets the next turn. You might use objects like a hose nozzle, a paper clip, a rubber band, a key, a battery, a staple remover, or a cassette tape. For younger children you may just have them guess what it is they feel and then allow the next child to have a turn.

Talk about all the different kinds of things we use in life to help us get a job done easier and faster.

Bible Story with Application:

Read Luke 10:20-37 and use the ideas you read, along with some of the following thoughts to tell the Bible story.

Since the story of the Good Samaritan is a common story, start by asking children what they know about it. This will prevent those who've heard it several times from tuning you out. Who can tell me what a Good Samaritan is? Allow children to recite the story or tell what they know about it. Why did Jesus tell that story? Again, allow children to share what they know.

The story of the Good Samaritan was told by Jesus to help people know what it means to be a good neighbor. A good neighbor doesn't just think about himself and the things he has to do, but he thinks about others, even people he doesn't know. He looks for ways to help them. Did you ever help someone you didn't know? Sometimes we gather up clothes we've outgrown and put them in the bin near the grocery store. Other times, you might give money to a person or an organization in need. Those are some ways you might help someone else.

In the story, Jesus told about a man who was traveling on a trip through a dangerous part of the country. He was on his way to Jericho. On his way, some bad men came and robbed him and took his money and beat him up, leaving him hurt on the side of the road.

Pretty soon a priest came by. He was a religious man but when he saw the hurt man, he walked to the other side of the street around the man and kept going. A second man came walking by. He was a Levite, someone who also was chosen by God to work in the temple. He also walked around the man and kept going. Why do you think these men didn't stop to help? Brainstorm with the kids about it with answers such as, they were too busy, he wasn't their friend, they were selfish, or they might get dirty.

What do you think the hurt man was feeling? He was probably wishing that someone would stop and help him. Pretty soon another man came by. He was a Samaritan. Now the Jews didn't really like the Samaritans, but this man didn't care. This man

saw someone who needed help and so he stopped. The Samaritan bandaged up the hurt man's sores and put him on his own donkey. He then took the hurt man to an inn where he paid someone to take care of him.

Jesus was trying to teach the people that we should care about other people, even if we don't know them. Honor does that.

It gives more than what's expected. It shares with people and brightens their day. What are some ways that you can show honor to people you don't know? What about at the store?

- *You might act respectfully instead of being wild.*
- *You might smile and say hello to someone you've never met.*

What about at church or at school?

- *You might just talk with someone to be kind, or help someone who spills a drink, or pick up trash when you see it on the ground so that the workmen don't have to do it.*

What do you get out of giving to others like that?

What do you get for picking up some trash and putting it into the trashcan at the store parking lot? Nothing? Well, you do get one special thing. You get the satisfaction in your heart that you are doing what's right.

God loves honor. In fact, God loves it when we do more than what's expected. We may think that no one is watching and that nobody cares, but God does. Every once in a while, even though you don't know it, someone may see your kindness. You never know when you will need an act of kindness in your own life. That's why the Bible encourages us to treat others kindly. Here's our Bible verse for today:

Bible Verse:

Matthew 7:12, "Do to others what you would have them do to you."

Prayer:

Lord, teach us how to give to others and not just think about ourselves. Help us see ways that we can demonstrate acts of kindness. Teach us how to give in small ways every day. Amen.

Craft and Activity Time

15-20 minutes

Refrigerator Magnet

Supplies needed:

- Photocopy the houses onto card stock for each child.
- Two magnets for each child from the craft supply store.

Instructions:

Color the houses with markers. Cut them out carefully and glue them each to a magnet. Talk about where you will put one and then who you will give the other one to.

Activity

Offering Hospitality

Bring several household objects and divide them into boxes. Some may be from the kitchen like placemats, plates, silverware, cups and napkins. Others may be from the living room with coasters, mugs, a nice book to read, and slippers. Others might be from the bedroom like small pillows and blankets.

Give each group of children a box and encourage them to set up house and then get ready to invite people over. Take turns allowing groups to be both the hosts and the guests and discuss hospitality and how it is a way to show honor to others.

Session 7

Game

15-20 minutes

Leading the Blind

Have children divide into pairs. Hand out one blindfold to each pair. If you don't have blindfolds you can make them by cutting an old sheet into strips 30" long. Have children lead each other through a maze of chairs in the room. The goal is to guide the "blind" child through the maze without touching any of the chairs. With older children you might use words and voices only and no touching to make it a little more difficult.

Review the Bible verse and talk about how we treat others with gentleness, kindness, love, etc.

Snack

5-10 minutes

Have children finish decorating their cookies. Allow them to eat one and then wrap the other one in cellophane to give away to someone else. Talk about who they will give the decorated cookies to and how that person might feel.

Review and Close

5-10 minutes

Talk to the children about their neighbors. You might say, "Let's talk about the people that live next door to you or down the street. What are their names? Do they have animals or children? What color cars do they have? What other things can you tell me about your neighbors?"

In the Honor Club we are looking for ways to show honor to others. How might you treat your neighbor as special? How might you be able to help them? Brainstorm with the children about ideas of ways they can help other people? Ask children to help you clean up the room where you have met. You might say, "We've been talking about honoring others. I need a person who would be willing to clean off that table… Straighten those chairs… Wipe off that counter… Sweep that floor…" Let children help and then praise them for showing honor. Tell them that you're grateful that they are part of the Honor Club.

House Magnets

Instructions:

Photocopy this page onto white card stock. The page contains enough magnet art for three children. Decorate the houses with markers and then carefully cut them out. Glue them to the magnets and let the glue dry.

Dealing with Anger

Preparing Your Heart to Teach Session 8:

What kind of cues can you feel in your body that tell you that you're starting to get angry? Maybe it's a scrunched forehead or a heightened volume or pitch in your voice. Maybe it's tight shoulders and more quick movements or short comments. Once you've identified the cues that anger is increasing then you can see it earlier and take action before you react and hurt someone. James 1:19 encourages us to slow down our anger, "Everyone should be quick to listen, slow to speak and slow to become angry."

Honor does more than just manage anger however. Honor turns people into peacemakers. Peacemakers can see the anger in others before they react and then help to bring peace into that situation. Peacemakers look for things in common, not differences. Peacemakers seek to bring people together in agreement and look for solutions where everyone wins. They think of the needs of others and try to make everyone feel good. A peacemaker honors others and promotes harmony, bringing joy into the family. That's why Jesus said in Matthew 5:9, "Blessed are the peacemakers."

How are you doing at being a peacemaker? People usually approach conflict in one of two ways: avoidance or overpowering. On the one hand, some people run away at the least sign of tension. They take others' emotions too personally and retreat. On the other hand, some people only feel comfortable when they are in control so they dominate others with their own intensity. As you become more sensitive about your own emotions and those around you, you'll be able to help others reduce their anger as well. That's honor.

What Children Learn in Session 8:

Anger management is one of the biggest challenges children face. In this session children will learn to see their own anger and learn some steps for dealing with it. The story of Cain's anger with his brother reveals the tragedy of lack of control in a child's life. Furthermore, because honor adds to relationships, children will learn to see anger in others and explore ways to respond to them, thus becoming peacemakers.

A Summary of the Video Session 8:

This session focuses on the first of three roadblocks to sibling harmony — anger. A plan for anger management is presented, and then parents are reminded that honor means adding something more. In Matthew 5:9, Jesus talks about being a peacemaker. Children are encouraged to see their own anger coming on and deal with it appropriately, then look for ways to bring peace into relationships as well.
(parent training video series is optional)

Read Along in the Book, "Say Goodbye to Whining, Complaining, and Bad Attitudes... In You and Your Kids":

Pages 115-122 provide insights into sibling conflict. Anger is a major hindrance to harmony in family relationships. Children learn not only to manage their anger but to grow as peacemakers as well.

Welcoming Activity

5-10 minutes

For Younger Children: As children come in, direct them to the table where they can decorate "Peacemaker" buttons with crayons or markers. These buttons can be worn around the neck using some string or yarn.

For Older Children: Use the Seek and Find Puzzle sheet and ask children to find the heart qualities in the puzzle.

Together Time

15-20 minutes

Use the thoughts and ideas below along with your own thoughts and the Bible to show children that anger management and being a peacemaker are ways that we can live out honor in relationships.

Introduction:

Admire the Peacemaker buttons that the children made and remind them that members of the Honor Club are peacemakers.

Object Lesson:

Build a small volcano to demonstrate how trouble can erupt and spill all over. Use a small clear plastic cup and add approximately 1/3 c. of vinegar. "Let's imagine this cup of vinegar is a person who gets easily irritated. Whenever he doesn't get what he wants, he gets angry. Or whenever Mom says "no," he becomes mean. Talk about how bad it smells. When someone is angry, others can tell. Sometimes he looks just fine like this cup of vinegar but let's add something to the cup and see what happens. When Mom says "no" or Dad asks him to empty the trash, then this happens." Then add 1 Tbsp. of baking soda. Watch the eruption. Talk about how anger can erupt and spill out all over.

Bible Story with Application:

Read Genesis 4:2-12 and use the ideas you learn from the scriptures along with some of the thoughts that follow to tell the Bible story.

Everyone close your eyes for just a moment and I'm going to start a sentence and I want you to finish it. See if you can think of an answer. One thing that makes me angry is _____. One time I got really angry was _____.

Have several children share their responses out loud.

I want to tell you a Bible story today about the first brothers in the Bible. Can anyone tell me what their names were? Cain and Abel. Both Cain and Abel brought an offering to God. Abel brought a lamb and Cain brought some fruit. In God's plan the lamb was a very special sacrifice, so, God didn't accept the fruit that Cain brought. This made Cain angry. He was very mad. God could tell that Cain was angry because God knows what's in our hearts.

Cain's face also showed that he was angry. Who can show me an angry face? How else can you tell when you're getting angry?

List several of the ways that people can tell when anger is growing. Include things like: clenched fists or teeth, breathing faster or more obviously, frowning, furrowed eyes, shoulders up, squinting eyes, big eyes. Have children demonstrate what it looks like when a person gets angry.

When Cain was starting to get angry, God talked to him to try to get him to stop. If you find yourself starting to get angry, stopping is one of the things you can do. Everyone take a deep breath with me. That's one way that you can stop and settle down. But sometimes you're so angry that the best thing to do is just go into the other room for a while and settle down.

God warned Cain that if he didn't do what was right that sin was crouching at the door. In our hearts, sin is waiting to pounce on us and anger is one way that we feed it. So we need to be careful when we are starting to get angry.

One man from India was trying to explain this idea of anger to his children. He gave them this picture. "It's as if you have two dogs fighting inside your heart. The white dog is a peaceful dog and enjoys getting along with others. The black dog is a mean dog, always angry and hurting other people. How do you know which dog in your heart will win? It's the one you feed the most. If you feed the black dog by thinking bad thoughts and planning bad things or holding onto anger in your heart then the black dog wins. If you think kind thoughts and act kindly toward others, even when they're being mean to you, then the white dog wins.

The rest of the story about Cain is pretty sad. He got so angry that he hit his brother. That is very

sad. When people get so angry that they start hitting other people, that's not good. Cain's brother Abel died because Cain hit him. That's a sad story and God disciplined Cain by having him go and live somewhere else.

It's important for each of us to learn how to deal with our anger. Once we can deal with our own anger then sometimes we can even help others deal with their anger. That's being a peacemaker. Peacemaker looks for ways to help other people who are upset. Sometimes they help that person and that makes them feel better. Sometimes a peacemaker leaves an angry person alone so that they don't get more provoked and angry.

In the Honor Club we want to look for ways to help other people become less angry. That's an important part of what honor is all about. The Bible verse today helps us understand the importance of dealing with anger.

Bible Verse:

Proverbs 29:11 "A fool gives full vent to his anger, but a wise man keeps himself under control."

Prayer:

Lord, teach us how to manage our own anger. Please help us see anger in others and know how to respond in a helpful way. Thank you for forgiving us and loving us even when we do the wrong things. Amen.

★ ★ ★ ★ ★

Craft and Activity Time

15-20 minutes

Supplies needed:

- Photocopy and cut out the thermometer craft page for each child.
- 14" piece of 3/4" red ribbon for each child.
- 1 1/2" safety pin for each child.
- Photocopy of red and green glue-on signs.

Instructions:

Photocopy the thermometer craft for each child. Follow the assembly instructions on the stop sign page. Have ribbon thermometer prepared ahead of time and for younger children, have red and green shapes cut out. Allow children to glue the shapes on in their appropriate places.

Decrease "mercury" down to frustration by pulling down on the stapled end of the ribbon. Advance "mercury" up the thermometer by pulling up with the safety pin, progressing up through anger to rage. Discuss with the children

the advantages of keeping the "mercury" as low as possible. Anger Management helps to prevent progression up the thermometer.

Talk about the signs of frustration and anger building, the importance of stopping to settle down, and then discuss three helpful choices.

Talk About It means discuss the problem with the other person in a reasonable and rational way. Use words like "I don't like it when you do that," to begin a discussion. *Get Help* means to go to a parent, teacher, or another adult for assistance in solving the problem. *Slow Down and Persevere* means to step back and readjust your expectations, then proceed calmly. When children are frustrated or angry, they should chose one of these three options.

Activity
Emotion Charades

For Older Children: Create cards that contain several emotions. Have the children take turns acting them out. After the rest of the group guesses which emotion the child was acting out, then ask the question, "What emotion did you see? How can you tell? The idea is that there are

cues we give off that reveal our emotions. Talk about the cues. Here are some suggestions for the cards: Love, surprise, excitement, hate, anger, sad, or happy.

For Younger Children: Younger children may not be in tuned with their emotions enough to act something out so be prepared to act most of them out yourself. These children will more readily detect emotions, making the activity a fun and insightful one. For the youngest children you may limit the emotions to sad, mad, and glad.

Game

15-20 minutes

Play the game - hot potato. The leader turns away from the group while the group, sitting in a circle, passes an object around the circle. When the leader says "hot potato," the passing stops and the person left holding the "hot potato" is out. Talk about how anger is like a hot potato in that it often causes a person to miss out on the joy of life.

Review the Bible verse using the idea of a vent to illustrate how some people handle anger.

Snack

5-10 minutes

Create traffic lights out of graham crackers, M&Ms and icing. Talk about how we can stop being angry by putting on the brakes, just like a car. We also want to learn to go and be a peacemaker.

Review and Close

5-10 minutes

Pet peeves are things that regularly irritate you or make you angry. You might begin by sharing a

couple of your own such as, "I get irritated when I get in the shower and someone flushes the toilet somewhere else in the house." Or "One thing that makes me angry is when someone leaves dirty dishes in the living room." Have children share their pet peeves. They might suggest that it makes them mad when someone moves the book they were reading, or when someone sits in their favorite seat, or when they're trying to watch TV and someone gets in the way. Then talk about how tolerance and forgiveness apply to pet peeves.

Welcoming Activity
Peacemaker Buttons
Instructions: Cut out and use a hole punch to put a single hole in each. This page has enough buttons for five children.

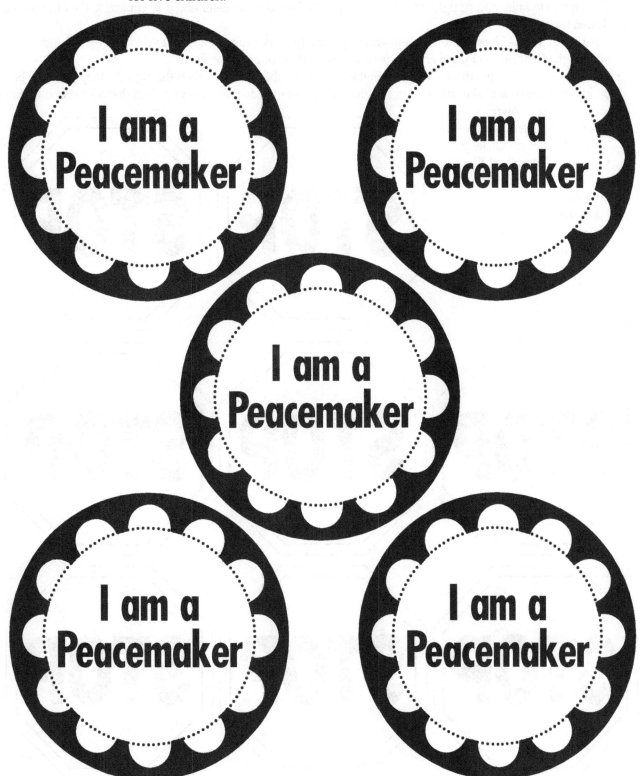

Anger Craft

Instructions: Photocopy this page onto red construction paper. This page contains enough signs for eight children.

- Photocopy the thermometer page onto card stock for each child.
- Use an exacto knife and straight edge to cut the sides of the thermometer and a 1" cut across the bulb on the dotted lines.
- Cut ribbon into 14" lengths, fold in half and staple the two ends together. Feed folded end up through the back of the bottom slit of the thermometer bulb and pull through to the front.
- Slide an open safety pin through one slit in the back of the thermometer, then through the loop of the ribbon, and back through the other slit. Fasten the pin and hold it to slide the ribbon up. Pull the stapled end to move the "mercury" down.
- Cut out stop signs and green, "Better Response" circles for younger children and allow older children to cut out their own.
- Have the children glue one stop sign and three "Better Response" circles onto their craft.

Instructions: Photocopy onto green construction paper. This page contains enough "Better Response" circles for six children.

TALK ABOUT IT

GET HELP

SLOW DOWN AND PERSEVERE

TALK ABOUT IT

TALK ABOUT IT

GET HELP

SLOW DOWN AND PERSEVERE

GET HELP

TALK ABOUT IT

GET HELP

SLOW DOWN AND PERSEVERE

SLOW DOWN AND PERSEVERE

TALK ABOUT IT

GET HELP

SLOW DOWN AND PERSEVERE

TALK ABOUT IT

GET HELP

SLOW DOWN AND PERSEVERE

Anger is Good for Identifying Problems but Not Good for Solving Them!

1 • Recognize it   2 • Stop to Settle Down   3 • Choose a Better Response

Rage

Anger

Frustration

Seek and Find Puzzle
Be a Peacemaker

Instructions:

Find the words in the boxes below. They can go in any direction: horizontal, vertical, or diagonal; forward, or backward. Draw a circle around each word.

HEART   PEACEFUL   HONOR

PROVOKE   ANGER   PEACEMAKER

RELATIONSHIP FOOL   FORGIVENESS

CONTROL   EXPLOSION

R	Z	X	C	V	R	E	K	A	M	E	C	A	E	P
E	P	B	N	M	A	S	D	F	G	H	J	K	L	S
L	E	W	H	E	C	R	T	Y	U	I	O	P	Q	S
A	A	Z	O	X	O	C	V	B	N	N	M	A	S	E
T	C	D	N	F	N	G	H	J	O	K	L	Q	W	N
I	E	E	O	R	T	T	Y	I	U	I	O	R	P	E
O	F	Q	R	W	R	E	S	R	T	Y	E	U	I	V
N	U	O	P	Z	O	O	X	C	V	G	B	N	M	I
S	L	A	S	D	L	F	G	H	N	J	K	L	Q	G
H	W	E	R	P	T	Y	U	A	I	F	O	O	L	R
I	O	P	X	Z	X	C	P	R	O	V	O	K	E	O
P	H	E	A	R	T	V	B	N	M	A	S	D	F	F

Not Having to be First All the Time

Preparing Your Heart to Teach Session 9:

If you were one of the stewards in the parable of the landowner in Matthew 25:14-30, how many talents might he give to you? He gave five talents to one, two to another, and one to the third. The scriptures say that he gave the number of talents based on the steward's ability. Too much responsibility would overwhelm, and giving too little would not sufficiently challenge.

We are all different and the amount of resources given to each person reflects this idea in life, but in some ways we can all identify with the man who received two talents. What do you think he thought as the talents were apportioned? "Hey, he got more than me," or "I'm pretty good. I got more than he did."

In part, faithfulness means to be content with the amount of responsibility we've been given and then to use it to the fullest. Some people feel bad because they don't have as much as someone else, while others are proud because they think they have so much. Take a few moments and reflect on the resources that God has given you and thank him for them. Evaluate your faithfulness to God with what you have already. Ask God to show you what it means to be faithful with what he's given you.

What Children Learn in Session 9:

Children love to be first or best and often measure their self worth that way. Although it's tempting to want to be the best, honor means that we learn to be servants. In this session children will hear the story in the Bible of two men who wanted the best seat. Jesus used that incident to teach his disciples the same message children need to hear today, how to think differently about being first or best.

A Summary of the Video for Session 9:

Selfishness or "wanting to be first or best" is one of the greatest enemies of honor. Two guys who wanted the best seat approached Jesus. His answer was, "Whoever wants to become great among you must be your servant." This session helps parents develop servant attitudes in their children. In particular the common complaint children raise is "That's not fair." Parents learn that fair doesn't mean equal and that they can cut down on a lot of the competitiveness and comparison in children by treating them all uniquely as God does us. Several practical ideas are presented that help parents know how to teach children about servanthood.
(parent training video series is optional)

Read Along in the Book, "Say Goodbye to Whining, Complaining, and Bad Attitudes... In You and Your Kids":

Pages 122-128 talk about one of the roadblocks to sibling harmony: selfishness. Kids often want to be first or best. Of course, the solution is to learn servanthood but that's not easy to teach to children. Several practical suggestions equip you with ideas to teach children a different way of thinking about being first or best.

Session 9

Welcoming Activity

5-10 minutes

As children arrive have them go to the table and create a Helping Hand Headband. Children can trace their own hands onto colored construction paper to make 3 or 4 hands for themselves. Also have them cut two long strips of construction paper about two inches thick to be used as the headband. Staple the strips together to form a band and staple the hands to the band. Talk about ways to have helping hands in the family. They can color the emblem and staple it on the front to say, "Kids Honor Club."

★ ★ ★ ★ ★ ───────────

Together Time

15-20 minutes

Use the thoughts and ideas below along with your own thoughts and the Bible to explain to the children that selfishness is a roadblock to good family relationships and that in the Honor Club we want to learn to serve others.

Introduction:

What are the kinds of people that make a school run smoothly? Encourage children to mention the different people including the principal, teachers, cook, cafeteria workers, hall monitors, crossing guards, janitors, repairmen, coaches, etc. What would happen if you had a school without a crossing guard? Or a school without teachers? What would it be like? Each of those people does a valuable thing for the school. They all help make it run smoothly. The same thing is true in a family. When each person adds to family life, then things go much better.

Object Lesson:

Have a bag of small individually wrapped candy, at least three pieces for each child. If you'd rather not use candy, pennies will also work.

Pour the bag on the floor in the middle of the circle of children and say, "You may take what you want but don't eat any yet." Then just watch what happens and don't interfere except to encourage people to take until it is gone. Whether it gets divided evenly or unevenly is not important in this stage. Greed, fairness, and selfishness may all be demonstrated.

Use this illustration to talk about selfishness and the importance of character. When people are alone and don't have limits spelled out for them, how do they act or respond? Be careful to talk in general terms and not single out any one child as an example.

Bible Story with Application:

Read Matthew 20:20-28 and the thoughts that follow to tell the Bible story. Emphasize the importance of being a servant with others.

One day two young men came to Jesus with a request. They wanted to sit in the best seat when Jesus started his kingdom.

What's your favorite seat in the car? What's your favorite seat at the table? What's your favorite seat when you're going to watch TV?
It seems that a lot of people fight to get the best seat or toy. Others fight because they want to be first. They want to be the first to receive a cookie, or first to be picked in a game, or first to choose an activity. Why do you think people tend to want to be first? It's usually because of selfishness.

How would you answer someone who came to you and wanted the best seat? Would you give it to him? Why or why not? What happens to a child who always gets what he wants?

Jesus knew that the request for the best seat came from selfishness. But Jesus also knew that being the best means more responsibility. The person on top, or the person who gets the most now has a greater ability to help others. Jesus knew that if these guys got the best seat without having the character to go with that responsibility, they would end up hurting others instead of helping them.

So, Jesus taught these disciples a very important lesson about life. He told them, "Whoever wants to become great among you must be your servant." That was an important lesson for both of those men to learn. What does it mean to be a servant? If two people both want to play on the same swing at the park, how does a servant

handle it? If they both want to go down the slide and they run fast to get to the ladder, how does a servant respond?

Are there any benefits that come to the person who lets someone else have the best seat or the first place? Sometimes the only benefit is the satisfaction in your heart that you know you did the right thing. Our Bible verse tells us Jesus' words about this issue.

Bible Verse:

Mark 9:35 "If anyone wants to be first, he must be the very last, and the servant of all."

Prayer:

Lord, teach us to serve others. Help us be willing to make others feel good instead of just wanting the biggest or best for ourselves. Teach us how to show honor to others. Amen.

★ ★ ★ ★ ★

Craft and Activity Time

15-20 minutes

Encouragement Arrows
Supplies needed:

- Plastic drinking straws, 3 for each child
- Photocopy of arrowheads and feathers for each child
- Scissors
- Markers
- Clear tape

Instructions:

Make a small slit in each end of each straw. Have children decorate the arrowheads and the feathers. Cut them out and slide them into the slit ends of the straw. Use a small piece of clear tape to hold them in place. Have children write their names on the feather end in small letters. Encourage children to say something kind every time they throw an arrow.

Discussion:

Talk about how we can send quick messages of encouragement to others by the way we talk, smile, or act toward someone else. You might even send an encouragement arrow in the form of a card or letter in the mail. Encouragement arrows build others up and help them become strong.

Activity

Teach children how to set a table properly with the cup just to the upper right of the plate, the fork on the left, and the knife and spoon on the right with the spoon on the outside. The napkin can be placed as decoration on the plate or folded under the fork. After children set the table in one place, have them go to another place and see if they can do it correctly. Encourage children to go home and help set the table. This is just one way that children can be helpful at home. You may have a brief brainstorming session about other ways children can help around the house.

Session 9

Game

15-20 minutes

Play "Mother May I" but replace words with "You can go first" and "No, you can go now." One person stands facing away from a line of kids. Then a child is either chosen at random, or in order, and gives and instruction. These follow a pattern, such as, "Brian, you may take 'x' giant/regular/baby steps forward/backward." The child responds with "You can go first." Mom then states "No, you can go now" and the child complies. If the child forgets to say "You can go first" he/she goes back to the starting line. First one to touch "Mother" wins.

Review the Bible verse and talk about what it means to be a servant.

Snack

5-10 minutes

Apple Delight

Cut up apples in 3/4 inch pieces. Put cinnamon in one salt shaker and sugar in another. Have children put about a 1/4 cup of apples into a small bowl or plate and sprinkle with the two ingredients and enjoy eating them. Talk about their favorite foods or favorite fast food restaurant. When it's time for the family to go out to eat, they might not get their first choice. How do they respond? You might say, "Can you enjoy going out to eat at another person's favorite place? If so, that's another way to be a servant."

Review and Close

5-10 minutes

Read the following story and then talk about how the people helped each other.

The Penny Auction

Years ago our country went through some very difficult times. We call those tough times the Great Depression. Many people were out of work and couldn't afford to keep their land, their houses, or their farms. Because some people owed money to the bank, they had to sell what they owned for a very low price. Can you imagine selling a horse for a quarter, or a tractor for a dollar? Things were so bad that people couldn't do anything else.

An interesting thing happened though. When it came time to sell the farm equipment, lots of people came but no one would bid on things. The tractor would sell for a dollar and a horse for a quarter. And then the person who bought it would turn around and give it back to the person that had to sell.

The people realized how much the farmers had lost and they had compassion on them. They were willing to help each other out in very difficult times. Someone could have come in and taken advantage of the situation and bought a lot of farm equipment cheap but they didn't. The people cared enough about each other to buy it at a very low price and then give it back to the other person. That showed honor to people who were hurting.

Encouragement Arrows

Instructions: Photocopy onto card stock. This page contains enough arrows for two children.

Instructions: Photocopy for each child to put on their Helping Hand Headband. This page contains enough emblems for six children.

Be Careful of Meanness

Preparing Your Heart to Teach Session 10:

What's one thing that you're good at? Maybe you're skilled at a sport, a game, or a craft. Or maybe it's a particular character quality like organization, friendliness, or compassion. In the Bible, the Hebrew word for wisdom is "hakam" which means "skill in life." The things you're good at reflect your ability to be wise in that particular area of life.

We all need to grow in wisdom. Sometimes it means knowing when to be quiet or when to speak up, how to raise a delicate issue, or having the insight to see the future consequences of current actions.

One of the benefits of knowing God is that he gives us the privilege to come to him and ask for wisdom. James 1:5 tells us that if we lack wisdom, we can ask God. Spend a few moments thinking about the areas where you need more wisdom in life. Maybe it has to do with your finances, a difficult relationship, or a personal struggle. Pray that God will grow you in those areas and then look for opportunities to trust him more. Wisdom is a treasure that God gives to his children.

What Children Learn in Session 10:

Children are often unkind or mean to each other demonstrating one of the three roadblocks to sibling harmony: foolishness. Meanness is just one example of foolishness and in this session children will learn from the Bible story of Joseph and his brothers. Foolishness happens when children don't recognize the consequences of their present actions. Children will learn that wisdom is the solution and how to develop it in their lives.

This lesson reviews the previous two lessons as well. Children are reminded about avoiding selfishness by playing the "There's Always Room for One More" game. The story about Harry Truman reminds children about the dangers of holding onto anger.

A Summary of the Video Session 10:

The third roadblock to sibling harmony is foolishness: the inability to see how present actions will result in negative consequences. Meanness is discussed because children who are mean don't realize the value of their brothers and sisters and don't see how their actions are damaging relationships. Parents learn to see foolishness in their children when kids say things like, "I was only kidding," or "I didn't mean to hurt him." The solution is to help children become wise. Excerpts from the book of Proverbs are shared to help parents see the importance and value of teaching children wisdom. Parents learn to address foolishness by teaching children to (1) take responsibility, (2) accept correction, (3) anticipate consequences, and (4) avoid meanness.
(parent training video series is optional)

Read Along in the Book, "Say Goodbye to Whining, Complaining, and Bad Attitudes... In You and Your Kids":

Pages 129-134 focus on the problem of foolishness in children. Foolishness doesn't recognize the consequences of current actions and includes things like meanness, talking too much, silliness, and reckless or dangerous play. The solution for foolishness is wisdom.

Welcoming Activity

5-10 minutes

Teachers could wear construction hats to tie into the theme of roadblocks. You might obtain some construction materials such as cones, signs, and flashing lights to decorate the room and hall as children arrive. Children come in to the tables ready to make paper bag vests that would be in the theme of Joseph's coat of many colors. Take a paper bag and cut out a circle for the neck and two arm holes on the sides. Cut the bag up the middle. Turn the bag inside out and have children color it with many colors.

Together Time

15-20 minutes

Use the thoughts and ideas below along with your own thoughts and the Bible to help children understand that acting in a mean way to others is foolish. In the Honor Club we want to grow in wisdom.

Introduction:

Have you ever seen men building a house? Laying cement? Digging up the street? Working on the power lines? Do you think you'd like to do that work when you get older? Have you ever seen construction on the road when you are driving? Sometimes the construction blocks the road and makes a problem. We're going to talk about another kind of roadblock today.

Object Lesson:

How many of you like to be tickled? How many of you don't like to be tickled? How many of you like to be tickled a little bit but not too much? One thing that helps know when it's too much is the Stop Rule. The Stop Rule in a family tells everyone else when the game is over. Who would like to show us the Stop Rule? I need two people, one to be the tickler and the other to be tickled. Have two children come up and have one start tickling and the other say "Stop." How would

you feel if you said stop and the other person didn't listen? Then it's not fun anymore. Now it's getting mean, right? We're going to see an example of meanness in our story today.

Bible Story with Application:

Read Genesis 37 and 45. Use the ideas from those passages and the thoughts below to tell the Bible story. Teach the children that meanness is foolish because it doesn't consider the future consequences.

Joseph was seventeen years old. One day he came home and told his dad about the bad things his brothers were doing out in the field. How do you think that made the brothers feel? They didn't like it. In fact they were very mad at Joseph. Instead of changing and doing the right things, they continued to do what was wrong.

Jacob was Joseph's father and he loved Joseph very much so he made him a special coat with many colors. There was no other coat like that? How do you think that made the brothers feel? They started getting angry in their hearts with Joseph.

Joseph had a dream about how he was going to be great someday, even greater than all his brothers and even his parents. How do you think that made Joseph's brothers feel? They were not happy at all.

Sometimes brothers and sisters get benefits that you don't get. They may get picked to play on a sports team or they may be good at playing a musical instrument. Sometimes when we see brothers or sisters getting something good, we feel jealous. We wish we could have those things. We have to be careful about those jealous feelings because they can lead to meanness.

I think that Joseph was irritating to his brothers. Joseph didn't seem to be sensitive to how his brothers felt when he acted. Sometimes brothers or sisters can be irritating and we have to be careful we don't get angry or hurtful with them. If we do, then we start to be mean. And that's exactly what happened to Joseph's brothers. They became mean.

Meanwhile for many years the brothers had to live with the knowledge that they had been mean to their brother. They didn't know what happened to him. How do you think they felt? I'm sure they felt very bad and at times I think they may even have wished that they hadn't been so mean to him.

God had a plan and he worked it out in a very special way. Later in their lives, God brought Joseph and his brothers back together. The brothers thought that Joseph would be mean back to them but he wasn't. Joseph didn't want to become ugly inside so he never treated his brothers with the same kind of meanness he had received from them.

Joseph's brothers were a long way from home. Joseph came to visit them and bring them some food. They saw this as an opportunity to be mean to their brother. No one would know so they tied him up and put him in a big pit. They were going to just leave him there and let him die. One of the problems with being mean is that you start to think of more and more ways to hurt people. You end up becoming an ugly person inside because you are doing mean things to others. Don't become a mean person, because if you do, then the problem gets worse and worse and worse inside you and pretty soon you won't even like the kind of person you've become.

Well, as Joseph's brothers sat there eating their lunch, they saw a caravan come by. This caravan bought and sold things and traveled around from country to country. That gave the boys an idea. They decided they would sell their brother and get some money for him. And that's exactly what they did.

But God was with Joseph and when the caravan got to Egypt one of the leaders bought him to be his servant. Joseph was a good worker and pretty soon he became an important leader in the country. Joseph was hurt by his brothers and what they did, but he never got angry in his heart. He forgave them.

Meanness is an example of foolishness. Foolishness is not recognizing the future results of our present actions. Meanness is so hurtful because it damages relationships more than we ever realize. The solution, of course, is to learn to be wise. A wise person knows that it is better to be kind and thoughtful to others. That's what our verse in the Bible tells us this week.

Bible Verse:

Proverbs 13:20 "He who walks with the wise grows wise."

Prayer:

Lord, teach us how to relate to others without meanness. Help us to see how foolish it is to be mean and how meanness turns us into ugly people. Give us the patience to deal with people who are irritating to us. Help us to be wise. Amen.

Craft and Activity Time

15-20 minutes

Instructions:

Photocopy a Roadblocks craft onto card stock for each child. Use an exacto knife to make six slits on the dotted lines.

Photocopy onto cardstock the anger, foolish, and selfish strips for each child. Cut them apart so that each child gets one of each.

Feed each strip through the slits in the Roadblocks craft. Start from the back, cross over the path on the front and go back through the second slit to the back.

Each strip should slide back and forth to reveal the roadblock (i.e. anger) and then the solution (i.e. peacemaker).

Allow the children to color the craft.

Activity

- Reenact parts of the story of Joseph. Here are some ideas of scenarios you might present and allow the children to finish the story. The scripts are found below. Photocopy this page so older children can read the scripts.

For Younger Children: You can read the scripts yourself and enjoy discussing them with the children.

The script will give children some ideas. Allow the students to improvise on how they would use anger, selfishness, or foolishness and then you can discuss how this is wrong.

- One script acts out how Joseph would have responded to his brothers if he was angry. How might a peacemaker handle it differently?

- The second script acts out how Joseph would have responded to his brothers if he was selfish. How might a servant handle it differently?

- The third script acts out how Joseph would have responded to his brothers if he was foolish. How might wisdom handle this differently?

★ ★ ★ ★ ★

Scripts for Joseph Role Plays

If Joseph were angry he might say:

I can't believe you guys! First you leave me there to die, and then you sell me to those slave traders. This is ridiculous! Who do you think you are? What do you think you're doing? Why I should just have my servants cut your heads off now!

If Joseph were selfish he might say:

I'm not going to help those guys. I don't need them. They are worthless and I am great. Who cares what happens to them. I can't be bothered. I have my own life now. I just need to think about all the things I need to do to run this country and those guys can fend for themselves.

If Joseph were foolish he might say:

What can I do to get back at those guys? I know, I could put holes in their water bottles so all their water drains out on the way across the desert. Or, I could send my raiding party out after them and just scare them to death. Revenge, that's what I want. What is some other kind of mean thing I could do to them?

Snack

5-10 minutes

Make butter by shaking heavy cream until it becomes solid. This fun activity teaches children about the consequences of shaking cream and teaches them where butter comes from. Start by purchasing two small containers of whipping cream. Bring a knife and some salt and some crackers or bread to spread the butter on.

Give the boxes of whipping cream to two children and tell them to shake them up. Pass the boxes around, encouraging several children to help. After 5-7 minutes of active shaking, the cream hardens into butter. Pour off the little bit of "buttermilk" and it's ready to eat. Be sure to add a little salt to the butter for flavoring and allow children to spread it on the crackers or bread.

Game

15-20 minutes

Always Room for One More

This game is similar to Musical Chairs except instead of getting people out, we just crowd them closer together. Fold several pieces of newspaper into fourths and place them on the floor, one less than the number of children playing. Allow a tape-player to play some music and when the music stops everyone has to stand on a paper. More than one person can stand on each paper. After each turn take away one paper. Children will have to stand on fewer and fewer pieces of paper as the game continues. You may need to open up the newspaper to accommodate all the children. In the end the kids enjoy trying to get everyone on one piece of newsprint.

Talk about kindness and sharing. In Kenya they have a saying that allows over 20 people ride in one minivan to get from one place to another. They say, "There's always room for one more!"

This game reminds children of the dangers of being selfish and about the need to share with others.

As you start, you may ask children, "Where do you think butter comes from?" Some children will give some pretty funny answers.

Homemade butter is creamy and soft and tastes quite nice so make sure you have enough of it for the whole class.

Discussion:

Foolishness doesn't recognize consequences of present actions. When you shake cream you get butter. What would happen if you...

...only ate candy and soda?

...never washed your clothes?

...didn't listen to your parents?

...were mean to people all the time?

Tie in the Bible verse here about learning wisdom in life.

Review and Close

5-10 minutes

Allow children to give examples of overcoming the three roadblocks to sibling harmony at home. If time permits allow children to role play real life situations.

Specific Ideas and Suggestions:

- **How can I be a peacemaker?**
  - Look for ways to compromise
  - Look for things in common
  - Look for ways to take turns

- **How can I be a servant?**
  - Look for things others need or want
  - Offer to help before being asked
  - Let others have the first turn or the best piece

- **How can I be wise?**
  - Listen before speaking
  - Think about consequences before acting
  - Accept correction with a good attitude
  - Apologize for mistakes

Read the following story about Harry Truman.

The Story of Harry Truman

It was just one of those afternoons. In one room, Jack was angry with Karen, "You broke my tape," he yelled. "I didn't break it, it just broke. It was old and just wore out. It wasn't my fault." "It was your fault," continued Jack. Jack was 15 and Karen was 13 and Karen had borrowed Jack's tape and it got stuck in the tape player. Jack picked up one of Karen's tapes and stormed out the door. Karen, crying with rage, ran to her mother but Mom was scolding their sister Mary for wearing her muddy shoes into the house and getting dirt all over the rug. Ten minutes later, Dad, came into the house with a scowl on his face. "I'm sick and tired of doing more than my share of work at the office," he muttered. "If there's anything I need tonight, it's peace and quiet."

What do you think the problem is here, boys and girls? Everyone is angry in the family. What happens when everyone is angry? People get hurt and they hurt others.

After a few minutes each member of the Jones family started getting involved in something else. Mom started cooking dinner again although she was still frustrated with Mary because of the dirt. Jack was in his room listening to his music. Karen was in the living room although she was still mad at Jack for taking her tape. Dad was reading the newspaper which was helping him get his mind off of work. But anger was still there.

That evening Grandpa and Grandma were over after dinner and the whole family was sitting around eating strawberry shortcake. Boy was it good. Dad was the first one to bring it up. "We sure had a hard afternoon as a family today," he said. Everyone was quiet. "I think a lot of us got pretty angry. What do you think we ought to do about it?" he continued. Mom said, "Yeah, I got pretty angry with you Mary. I shouldn't have yelled like that." Mary said, "I'm sorry Mom for getting mud on the rug." Karen looked down, so did Jack. "It looks like you two are still pretty angry with each other," Dad said.

Grandpa said, "I have a story I think you might like." Everyone liked Grandpa's stories. He often had a way of telling stories that helped with every day life. Even though Jack was 15 years old, he hadn't grown out of the stories that Grandpa told.

"A few years ago there was a mountain in Washington called Mount St. Helens. People lived around the mountain in homes they had built. Farms were there. Motels and lodges contained many people who would come up the mountain for a vacation. One man owned a lodge. His name was Harry Truman. He had 16 pet cats on his lodge.

One day scientists saw that earthquakes were happening on this beautiful mountain. They knew what that meant. This mountain, that used to be a volcano, was about to erupt again. They waited, and more earthquakes came and pretty soon a hole appeared in the top of the mountain and gas and ash shot up high into the sky. It was then that they decided to get everyone out of there. They went around and told everyone that the mountain was about to blow up. People started leaving but one man, Harry Truman said no. He didn't believe the mountain would blow up. I can handle this, he said to himself and to others.

So, Harry Truman stayed up on the mountain and just a few weeks later, it blew up, and blew up big. Harry Truman died on that mountain. Why did he die? He died because he didn't see the warning signs and he didn't believe that the damage would hurt him."

So, what does that have to do with our problem here, Dad said to Grandpa?

"I believe anger is like that mountain,"Grandpa answered. "There are warning signs that all of us have that anger is approaching quickly. If we don't do something about it then we and usually others can get hurt. Anger damages relationships and the person who gets hurt the most is the person who is angry. He is unhappy and not at peace with himself or others. Anger can be a damaging thing but much of it can be prevented if we will only discover the early warning signals and take action earlier in the process."

As Karen listened she realized that what Grandpa was saying was true. She said, "I sure don't like being angry. I feel all upset inside. I like being peaceful." The Jones family decided that they would work on seeing anger earlier and trying to take steps to prevent it from becoming hurtful in their family.

3 ROADBLOCKS TO HONOR

HONOR in my House!

Roadblocks Craft Strips

Instructions: Photocopy this page onto card stock. This sheet contains enough strips for two children.

KEY:

✂ ——— Cut

- - - - Fold

Peacemaker

ANGER

Wise

FOOLISH

HeLpfuL

SELFISH

KEY:

✂ ——— Cut

- - - - Fold

Peacemaker

ANGER

Wise

FOOLISH

HeLpfuL

SELFISH

Responsibility and Privilege

Preparing Your Heart to Teach Session 11:

What's an example of a time when you lost a privilege because you didn't handle the situation well? Maybe you lost the freedom of not paying interest because you didn't pay your credit card bill by the due date, or your car got damaged because you didn't do the proper maintenance.

The opposite is also true. Can you think of a time when you received a privilege because you were responsible? Maybe you received a promotion at work or an award for doing well.

Privilege and responsibility go together in life. When the landowner in Jesus' parable in Matthew 25:14-30 returned to see how the stewards had done, he rewarded two of them by saying, "Well done, good and faithful stewards, because you have been faithful with a few things, I will put you in charge of many things." When we demonstrate responsibility, we receive privileges.

Pray and evaluate with the Lord the responsibilities and privileges he's given you. Let the Lord commend you for your faithfulness so far and challenge you to greater faithfulness before him.

What Children Learn in Session 11:

One important principle in life is that privilege and responsibility go together. Many times children want privileges but aren't responsible enough to handle them. Through the parable of the landowner and the stewards, children will learn how their current demonstrations of responsibility will determine whether they get privileges in the future.

A Summary of the Video Session 11:

Family life changes when children become teenagers. The causes and purpose of these changes are discussed in this session. Parents are encouraged to make the Teenage Parenting Shift. A helpful discipline technique is presented from the parable of the talents (Matthew 25). When the landowner returned he rewarded the servants who were responsible by giving more privileges. That principle can be applied to teens as the primary discipline technique: Privilege and responsibility go together. Parents are encouraged to use honor to build bridges with teenagers.
(parent training video series is optional)

Read Along in the Book, "Say Goodbye to Whining, Complaining, and Bad Attitudes... In You and Your Kids":

Pages 137-164 talk about applying the concept of honor to the parent/teen relationship. Special consideration is given to helping teens understand how privilege and responsibility go together.

Session 11

Welcoming Activity

5-10 minutes

Cut pieces of construction paper into several sized geometric shapes. Small and large rectangles, squares, ovals, circles, and triangles. Have children glue the shapes onto a piece of construction paper to form a pet. They may create a dog out of ovals and circles or a mouse out of triangles or a horse out of a combination of shapes.

For Older Children: You might have them draw a pet and be prepared to share about it.

★ ★ ★ ★ ★ ────────────

Together Time

15-20 minutes

Use the thoughts and ideas below along with your own thoughts and the Bible to talk about the connection between privilege and responsibility.

Introduction:

Have children show their shape animals and talk about funny names you could give them. Ask children about their pets and use the opportunity to talk to kids about what responsibilities go with having a pet.

Object Lesson:

Bake a batch of cookies but leave out the sugar. You only need enough for each children to have a half or quarter of a cookie. Then add sugar and bake the rest to be used for snack later in the session. Pleasantly ask children if they'd like a piece of a cookie from a new recipe that you tried. Of course the children will be eager at first and then surprised when they take a bite. "I think I must have left out an ingredient. What do you think it was?"

"What would you think if you told me to bake cookies for your party and this is what I gave you? You'd probably be pretty disappointed wouldn't you. You probably wouldn't give me that job again. You might even say that I wasn't very responsible at making cookies."

Bible Story with Application:

Read Matthew 25:14-30. Use the ideas you learn and the thoughts that follow to teach children the importance of being responsible and how privilege and responsibility go together.

One day a man went on a trip but he needed to have someone take care of his things. Have you ever helped someone by taking care of their things while they were gone on a trip? Maybe you fed and walked the dog, or brought in the mail or the newspaper, or you watered the plants.

This man went on a longer trip than that and so he turned over part of his business to three people. He gave them each a different part of the job and different amounts. To one man he gave five talents. A talent was a sum of money. Another man got two talents and a third got one. The reason the man gave different amounts is because the servants had different abilities and could only handle what was given to them.

After a while the man came back from his long trip. He came to check on the servants to see how they had done with the money he had given them. The first servant who had received five talents had gone to work right away and now had five more talents to give to the man. He had done a good job. The second man also did well. He immediately went and worked with the money he had received and he earned two more talents. The owner was very pleased. He had given the jobs out and the servants were responsible with the jobs. He decided to reward them by giving them more privileges. He said, "Because you were faithful in a few things, I will put you in charge of many things."

That very same thing happens in life a lot. Let me tell you a story about Jack. Jack's neighbor asked him to take care of his mail and newspapers while he was gone and to water his plants. When the neighbor returned, he was pleased to see that Jack had done just as he asked. He not only paid Jack for doing the work but he also told him that he could have the job of mowing his lawn. Jack was thrilled. This was another way that he could earn some money.

Privileges come to people who are responsible. When you can be honest and do the right thing at home then Dad or Mom feel comfortable allowing you to go over to a friend's house. If you can do the right thing when parents aren't watching, then Mom or Dad might let you stay home by yourself when they go next door or to the store for a few minutes. Privilege and responsibility go together. That's why it's so important to do the right thing, treat people kindly, be honest, and finish jobs you start. The things you do now will determine what privileges you get in the future.

The story about the man who went on a trip has one sad part to it. The third servant wasn't responsible. In fact, he was lazy and so he didn't do anything with the talent he was given. In fact, all he could do was give excuses instead of being responsible. So, he lost privileges and his privileges were given to someone else. That's what happens in life too. If you aren't responsible with what you have now, you will lose privileges.

Our Bible verse today talks about the importance of being faithful with the responsibilities we now have. As members of the Honor Club we want to be responsible children and adults.

Bible Verse:

Matthew 25:23 "You have been faithful with a few things; I will put you in charge of many things."

Prayer:

Lord, teach us how to be faithful with the responsibilities we have already. Help us to see the privileges we enjoy instead of taking them for granted. Give us the ability to be responsible with the things you've given to us. Amen.

Craft and Activity Time

15-20 minutes

Privilege and Responsibility Craft Worksheet

Photocopy the activity sheet and let children decorate the picture with crayons or markers. Encourage the older children to write privileges and responsibilities that they have. Brainstorm as a group as kids are writing to give them a lot of ideas.

For younger children, talk about what a responsibility and a privilege are. Give examples that they can understand and help them see that the two are tied together.

Activity

For Younger Children: Use the leftover shapes from the craft earlier. You may want to make more shapes for the children. First, sort by shape, putting all the circles together, the triangles in the next pile or use baskets and so on. Then redistribute the shapes and have children

sort them by color. Then, if you have time, have the children sort them by size. Talk about sorting mail. "Sorting the mail is not an easy job. The mail carrier has to take the mail and put it all in order before he goes out in his truck to deliver it to all the homes. We're going to pretend that we are mail carriers and put the mail in these five baskets. We will use these colored shapes as the mail."

For Older Children: Gather together several common objects for this activity. Include things like a basketball, a coat, a book, a tennis ball, a plate with a cookie on it, and other miscellaneous things you have around. Give children many objects to make the task very difficult but not impossible. "You've been given a special job to do. Here are your instructions. Carry the objects from here to the other side of the room in one trip." If it seems too easy then you might say, "Bill did a great job. We need someone else who can do it but we are going to add something new this time." Continue adding objects and see who can carry them all across the line in one trip without dropping anything.

In both activities, talk about being responsible to do the job right.

Game

15-20 minutes

The "Doing it Right" Game

Place index cards all over the floor between a starting point and an ending point in the room. These cards must be far enough apart to allow people to navigate through them but close enough to make it difficult. One child is blindfolded on one side of the room. The second child

stands at the finish line giving instructions about moving a little to the left or right or straight ahead. After you get this working well, you can have a second team working at the same time, further complicating the communication process. Young children can try to maneuver through with their eyes open but hopping on one foot or holding hands with a partner.

Review the Bible verse and talk about what it means to be faithful or a good friend.

Snack

5-10 minutes

Eat the good cookies that contain sugar. Talk about how these cookies are a little different than the previous ones. You might say, "Now, do you think you'd let me bake the cookies for your party?"

Review and Close

5-10 minutes

List some of the privileges children have as they were mentioned over this session. You might want to write a list on a whiteboard so children can see them. One of the signs of responsibility is that we are grateful for the privileges we have. Some children become demanding and view privileges as rights. These children eventually lose those privileges.

Gratefulness is being thankful for what I do have instead of complaining about what I don't have. Encourage children to be thankful. A sincere thank you can brighten a person's day. It can bring cheer into relationships.

What are some ways we can say thank you without words? Explore the ways kids can show gratefulness to their parents and others who have done something kind for them.

Responsibility and Privilege Go Together Craft

Instructions: Photocopy this page for older children. It will add to their craft. Have them list responsibilities and privileges. Then they can cut out these two rectangles and glue them onto the bridge page, one rectangle on each of the lower corners. Younger children can color the bridge page only.

RESPONSIBILITIES
I Have at Home

PRIVILEGES
I Have at Home

Responsibility and Privilege Go Together

PRIVILEGE

RESPONSIBILITY

What Signals Do You Give?

Preparing Your Heart to Teach Session **12**:

How would people characterize you? Would they say you are neat or messy? Active or quiet? Nervous or composed? Joyful or sad? Dominant or responsive? How do they know these things about you? What are the cues they see that reveal your inner self?

We all give cues to people that tell them more about what we are like and how we relate. Jesus told his disciples in John 13:35, "By this all men will know that you are my disciples, if you love one another." Jesus wanted his disciples to know that others are watching, and as they do, they're picking up cues that tell a lot about who we are.

When you begin to look at the cues you give to others, you may discover that they aren't representing the real person you want to be. Are you agitated in a discussion showing that you're not really interested in that person? Or maybe you take irritations out on someone demonstrating that the issue you're working on is more important than the person involved. The way you dress, give eye contact, and your voice tone and volume all give cues to others.

As you begin to evaluate those subtle signals, ask God to help you adjust them to demonstrate the kind of person he wants you to be.

What Children Learn in Session **12**:

Honor and dishonor are demonstrated in subtle ways through cues that many children aren't even aware of. Using the story of Paul and Silas in prison, children will learn how the things they do and say often tell a lot about who they are on the inside. Children will learn how to evaluate the honor cues they give to others. They learn that character is important and indicates what their heart really looks like.

A Summary of the Video Session **12**:

In this session the Network Factor is described, a tool used to change the way families interact. All relationships have predictable patterns. Some are helpful and others are not. Parents are taught to look closely at the patterns in their family and encouraged to target the relationships that need more honor. Triangling happens in relationships when two people in conflict draw another one into the fray. Triangling happens more than many parents realize. Using the Network Factor, parents learn to identify negative relating patterns and replace them with honoring ones.
(parent training video series is optional)

Read Along in the Book, "Say Goodbye to Whining, Complaining, and Bad Attitudes... In You and Your Kids":

Pages 65-88 discuss the Network Factor and apply it to family life. You will learn how to pinpoint the dishonoring patterns in relationships and know where to challenge your family to develop honor.

Welcoming Activity

5-10 minutes

Coat of Arms

Photocopy the Activity Sheet for this lesson and have it available for children as they come in. Children should draw pictures in the spaces provided of fun things that happen in their family. Some ideas may be swimming together, going out to eat, a picture of a pet, watching a movie, going to the park, church, camping, or just driving in the car. When children are finished they could cut out the Coat of Arms, write their name in the banner and cut it out, and then paste the two on a new piece of construction paper.

★ ★ ★ ★ ★

Together Time

15-20 minutes

Use the thoughts and ideas below along with your own thoughts and the Bible to help children see the cues that give out to tell others about themselves.

Introduction:

Talk to children about listening with both eye balls. Many children will think this is funny but looking at someone when they say their words is a way of showing that you're interested. You might say, "How many of you look at your mom or dad when they talk to you? Why? Or Why not?" Attentiveness is one of those qualities that children can learn and practice at home.

Object Lesson:

Just put your finger on your nose. Without using words, try to get another child to do the same. Keep your finger on your nose as you try to get all the children to follow suit. When you have all the children with their fingers on their noses, then say, "We did it! How did you know that I wanted you to put your finger on

your nose? I want you to be watching me the rest of today. I'm going to put my finger on my nose and we'll see if we can get everyone to do it without talking about it.

Bible Story with Application:

Read Acts 16:16-36. Use the ideas you learn from the story and the thoughts that follow to tell the Bible story, teaching the children about the signals they give that reveal what kind of a person they really are.

Paul was just trying to help. He healed a little girl who was possessed by a demon. But some of the townspeople didn't like it. They were able to make money off the fact that she was sick. They dragged Paul and Silas to the authorities. They wanted Paul and Silas thrown in jail right away. So that's what happened.

The jailer put Paul and Silas into the prison. It was dark and probably smelled bad. He put chains on their arms and locked the prison doors. Paul and Silas were stuck. I think that jailer had to listen to a lot of complaining and whining from prisoners over the years. I'm sure some prisoners were mad that they were in jail and they took it out on the jailer. But not Paul and Silas. They were different. The jailer could see that they didn't act like everyone else.

Instead of whining and complaining about being

in prison, all the other prisoners were quiet, listening to Paul and Silas singing songs to God. In fact, the way that these two men lived seemed very different to the jailer. He had never in his life seen anything like it. He began asking himself, "Who are these men and who is their God?"

About midnight, while Paul and Silas were still singing, there was an earthquake. How would you like to be inside a prison with your arms chained to a wall behind bars during an earthquake? You'd be stuck. You wouldn't be able to get out. That would be a scary experience, but Paul and Silas trusted God so even when things were scary, they responded differently than others would. The jailer was impressed.

The earthquake shook the ground and the prison doors came loose and the chains came off the prisoners. The jailer was afraid. He knew that if all the prisoners escaped, the authorities would be angry with him and would punish him. He decided to take out his sword and kill himself.

Just then Paul yelled, "Don't hurt yourself. We're all still here." The jailer couldn't believe it. Could it be? Why wouldn't Paul and the other prisoners just run out? But they didn't. Paul and Silas knew that God wanted to do something special in this jailer's heart. That evening the jailer accepted Jesus into his life. He wanted to be different than all the rest of the people he knew and he saw that Paul and Silas were different. The jailer wanted Jesus to change him as well.

The jailer brought Paul and Silas out of the prison to his house where he washed their wounds and took care of them the rest of the night. I wonder what they talked about. I'm sure that the jailer and his family were eager to grow in their relationships with God. Several years later, Paul was in another prison in Rome and he thought about the jailer and others who had become Christians in Philippi so he wrote them a letter and in it he said, "Conduct yourselves in a manner worthy of the gospel of Christ." (Philippians 1:27)

One of the reasons that the Philippian jailer became a Christian is because he saw that the way Paul and Silas lived was different. They gave off cues that said they didn't act the same as other people did. They didn't whine or complain about life. They didn't get angry and say mean things the way others did. All of those actions were little messages that told the jailer that these men were different.

What kind of cues do you give that tell what kind of person you are? Are you a whiner or complainer? Do you argue a lot? Are you kind and think of what would make others feel good? Those little messages you give by your actions tell people a lot about the kind of person you are.

Put your finger on your nose and see how long it takes children to see it and respond.

Our Bible verse gives us some ideas of how we can think of others.

Bible Verse:

1 Thessalonians 5:11 says, "Therefore encourage one another and build each other up, just as in fact you are doing."

Prayer:

Lord, help us see how the small things we do show people what we're really like. Teach us how to make the small things count so others can see you through our lives. Amen.

Craft and Activity Time

15-20 minutes

Encouraging Words Chain

Supplies Needed:

- Construction paper
- Tape
- Pens
- Scissors

Instructions:

Have each child cut 5-10 strips of construction paper of different colors about one inch wide and eight inches long. Have them write on the chain pieces words of encouragement like "Thank you," "Please," "I'm sorry," "Can I help you," "I like your shirt," "This is a great dinner," "I love you," "You are fun to be with," etc. With younger children, you could let them put encouragement stickers on. (Encouragement stickers may be found in any teacher store or school supply store. They say things like "good job" "well done" etc.) Tape or staple the ends together, interlocking them into a chain. Encourage children to take the chain home and hang it up somewhere as a reminder to say encouraging things to others.

Remind children that kids in the Honor Club encourage others.

Activity
Group Puzzle

For Older Children: Photocopy the puzzle verse at the end of this lesson onto cardstock. One puzzle for every 3 or 4 students. Cut the puzzle up into 8-12 pieces depending on the age of the children and put the pieces into an envelope. Divide the children into groups of three or four and give each group an envelope of puzzle pieces. Encourage the children to work as a team to put the puzzle together. Once assembled, have several children read the verse. Discuss how this verse applies to family life.

For Younger Children: Play the Simon Says game replacing "Simon" with "Mommy." Teacher says, "Mommy says turn around." If I don't say "Mommy says," then don't do it. One of the keys to obedience is to listen carefully.

End the game time by putting your finger on your nose and enjoy watching children see and respond.

Game

15-20 minutes

Choose a child to be "it." The rest of the class has to make this person laugh and the person who is "it" tries to not laugh. Children can make noise, tell jokes, make faces, anything. The only thing they can't do is touch the person — so no tickling! As you play, watch to see if you can guess when this person is about to loose it. Talk about what signals come before the laughter. Then take turns being "it."

Review the Bible story and talk about encouraging others.

Snack

5-10 minutes

Apple Faces

Give children sliced red apples, cake frosting, and mini-marshmallows. Each child can arrange two apple slices touch-ing each other with the peals to the outside (the lips). Next, put a narrow spread of frosting overlapping both apples on the place where they meet (the gums). Then put mini-marshmallows along the frosting (the teeth). Children can make and eat the smiley faces. Talk about how the Kids Honor Club focuses on being happy instead of whining and complaining.

★ ★ ★ ★ ★

Review and Close

5-10 minutes

Ask for a few volunteers to act out some emotions. See who can act the maddest and at the same time say, "I love you." Now look excited like you just opened a present and say, "I'm mad at you." Is that hard? The point? Sometimes we try to say something nice but we say it in such a grumpy way that it doesn't come out very nice. Attitude is so important. If you can have the right attitude, you'll be able to talk about even the most difficult things.

Therefore encourage one another and build each other up, just as in fact you are doing.

1 Thessalonians 5:11

Welcoming Activity Coat of Arms

Learning to Play on a Team

Preparing Your Heart to Teach Session 13:

We tend to take for granted things we once valued quite highly. One mom said, "I remember when we first got our new sofa. I wouldn't even let the kids sit on it. It's been years now and I laugh at how much use we get out of it." Unfortunately, the same thing is true of relationships in the family. We tend to take people for granted. One teenage boy observed that his mom treated the customers at work better than she treated him sometimes.

Jesus said the same thing in Mark 6:4, "Only in his hometown, among his relatives and in his own house is a prophet without honor." Honor seems to diminish over time in families if it isn't encouraged and developed. Are there some ways that you may have let your honor slip away in family life? What might be some ways that you could develop honor more?

The saying, "Familiarity breeds contempt," can be too true when it comes to family relationships. Pray and ask God for a few ways that you might treat each of your family members as special and show them honor this week. It may mean making an extra phone call or sending a card. Don't keep putting honor off. It's too important for nurturing healthy relationships.

What Children Learn in Session 13:

Parents want to have a cooperative working relationship with their children but unfortunately their children may not embrace the same goal. In this session, children will learn that all believers, including parents and children, are part of a new family. That means that we view each other as part of the same team. Children explore the idea of the family as a team and look for ways that they can contribute to a good team spirit.

A Summary of the Video Session 13:

Honor comes when we value each other. This session talks about viewing our children as brothers and sisters in Christ. When families grasp this truth, they see the tremendous value of children and parents. Several practical ideas are shared to help families grow closer together as a team. *(parent training video series is optional)*

Read Along in the Book, "Say Goodbye to Whining, Complaining, and Bad Attitudes... In You and Your Kids":

Pages 179-188 talk about how we view each other in family life. Fathers and mothers are really brothers and sisters to their children when family members have accepted Jesus into their lives.

Session 13

Welcoming Activity

5-10 minutes

Cut out pictures of family members from magazines. Bring a large assortment for the children to choose from. Photocopy the Family Portrait frame from the end of the lesson so that each child can have one. Have children glue the pictures they choose into the frame. Fill the child's last name into the blank space on the bottom of the frame.

Together Time

15-20 minutes

Use the thoughts and ideas below along with your own thoughts and the Bible to talk about how we are all brothers and sisters in Christ.

Introduction:

How many of you have ever gone to get a picture taken with your family? Did you get all dressed up? I want to tell you about a trick one store played on people to see what they would do. When people came to pick up their pictures the photographer had used a computer to take another person and put him right in the picture with the family. Can you imagine looking at a picture of your family and finding an extra person in the picture that you didn't know?

Then they asked the people if they would be interested in buying the picture. Of course, people said, "No, way. That person isn't a part of my family."

The photographer said, "Well maybe we could sell you the picture at a discount. Would you take it then?"

"No way," they continued. "That person is not a part of my family."

Finally, the photographer told them it was a joke and then brought out the real picture for them and they all laughed together about it.

Object Lesson:

Beforehand, cut string into 3' lengths, one piece of string for each pair of children. Tie the string into knots. For older children you may tie as many as 50 knots, but younger children may only be able to handle 3-4 loose knots. Divide the children into pairs. Give each team a knotted string and ask them to work together to untie it.

After the knots are undone, talk about problems. Did you feel like you wanted give up? How did you work together to solve the problem? Did only one person do all the work while the other watched?

Bible Story with Application:

Read Matthew 12:46-50 and use the ideas you read in the Bible and the following thoughts to tell the Bible story, teaching children that believers of all ages are part of the family of God.

I want to tell you another story that comes from the Bible. One day Jesus was helping a lot of people and the house they were in was crowded. In fact, it was so full that not even one more person could fit inside. Someone leaned over to Jesus and said, "Your mother and brothers are standing outside and want to speak with you."

Did you know that Jesus had brothers? What would it have been like to be a brother of Jesus growing up? Do you think that Jesus fought with his brothers and sisters? Do you think he yelled or said mean things? Do you think he shared his toys and helped his mom around the house? It's fun to think about that isn't it? Jesus loved his mother and brothers. In fact, when Jesus was on the cross dying, he took time to care for his mother and told his disciple, John, to take care of her.

But on this occasion Jesus wanted to teach the people something very important. He wanted to teach them that they have a spiritual family of brothers and sisters when they choose to follow him. Did you know that when you trust Jesus as your savior you enter a new family? God is the father and all the other people who have trusted Christ are your brothers and sisters. If you're a Christian and I'm a Christian, what does that make us together? It makes us brother and sister.

Why did Jesus want the people to know that? Because Jesus knew that if people would recognize this truth then they would treat each other differently. A family is a special thing and when we become Christians we join the family of God. That means that we need to learn how to get along with our new brothers and sisters in Christ. It means that we get to know our Heavenly Father.

It's fun to think about having a big family and getting to know everybody that way. But one of the nicest things is that if you and your parents are Christians then your mom and dad are your brother and sister in Christ. Now, that is a different thought. Isn't it?

Bible Verse:

Mark 3:35 "Whoever does God's will is my brother and sister and mother."

Prayer:

Lord, teach us to treat each other kindly. Help us to treat parents in kind ways as our brothers and sisters in Christ. Thank you for giving us a big family so that we can learn and grow. Amen.

Session 13

Craft and Activity Time

15-20 minutes

Create a Team Pennant

Photocopy the pennant onto card stock. Encourage children to draw pictures of their family or write their family name on the pennant and decorate the edges with the markers provided. Fasten the pennant to a plastic straw so children can wave it as a pennant.

Activity
The Communication Game

For Older Children: Pair up your students or have them work in small groups. One student of each group needs a pencil and paper while the other has a common object like a key or a soda can. The "drawer" is not to see the object but must draw it simply by following commands from the person holding the object. Afterwards talk about how communication can be difficult because what we think is clear, may be unclear for others.

Blind-Folded Follower Game

For Younger Children: Pair up children and have one wear a blind fold and have the other lead the first around the room. If children are ready you might have them use words instead of touch to communicate. After the game, sit down and talk about the value of team work, listening and following instructions. How do the pair of children work together? Talk about the value of teamwork in a family.

Game

15-20 minutes

Play "Untie the Human Knot" game. Group the children so that there are about 5-10 per group (the older the children, the larger the group can be). Have children form a circle and grab hands across the group, careful to not grab the hand of the person next to them and not grab two hands of the same person. After everyone is holding two different hands, the group must slowly "untie" itself until the children are all holding hands in a circle. No one is allowed to let go of a hand during the game. When completed, some children will be facing out while others are facing in. Adults should be quiet, allowing children to direct each other and figure out how to "untie the knot."

★ ★ ★ ★ ★

Snack

5-10 minutes

Provide a snack that one might eat at a ballgame or other sports event. This could be popcorn or soft pretzels or some other fun snack. Talk about how we root for our home team at a game and how we can root for one another in our families.

Review and Close

5-10 minutes

Have the children do some sort of task like building a tower or cleaning up the toys. Stress the importance of teamwork. Review the Bible verse and take time to thank each child for their participation in the Kids Honor Club. See if anyone can remember the definition of honor. You may want to give each child a small gift as a reminder that showing honor is like giving a gift.

Welcoming Activity: A Family Portrait

Instructions: Cut out pictures of family members from a magazine. Paste them inside the frame.
Write the last name of the family in the blank space between "The _____ Team."

The _____ Team

Team Pennant Craft

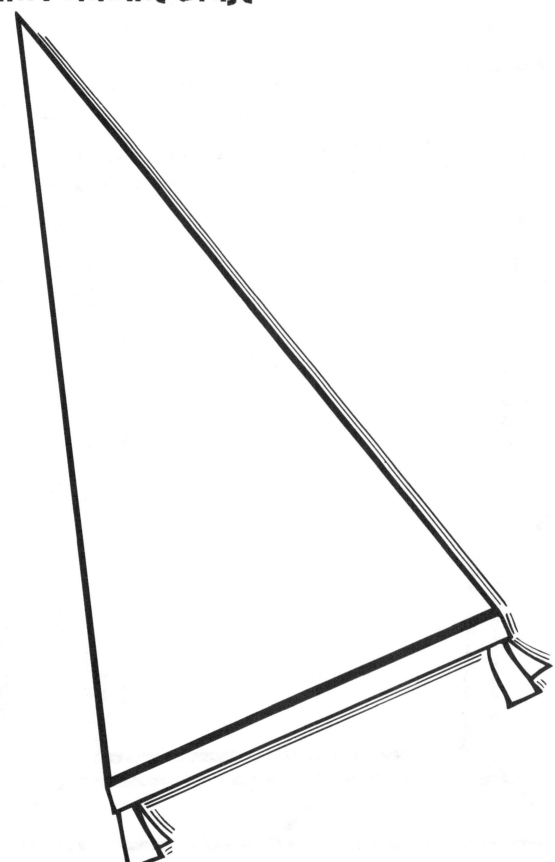

Photocopied by permission from the National Center for Biblical Parenting

Complete Honor Church Kit

This video series kit provides you with material for both the teaching component and the sharing time of your group meetings. The Leader's Guide includes fully-reproducible participant pages and questions for group discussion.

Includes the following:
- Thirteen 30-minute videos on 2 DVDs
- Kids Honor Club 13-session Children's Curriculum, 112 pages
- Video Series Leader's Guide with handouts and questions for group discussion, 44 pages
- Say Goodbye to Whining, Complaining, and Bad Attitudes...in You and Your Kids book, 230 pages

Plus:
- Parenting Seminar Outreach Manual, 74 pages
- Parenting Seminar Resource CD with advertising materials.

This video series talks about the concept of honor in very practical terms. Learn how to teach children to add energy to family life instead of draining it. Three of the sessions focus on sibling conflict directly, but all the sessions deal with family relationships and how honor can change the way you relate. This series is for parents of children ages 2-18.

Honor Family Kit

Using drama, stories, humor, and scripture, Dr. Scott Turansky and Joanne Miller share practical ways to address some of the most common problems in family life. Filmed before a live audience of parents and teens, these practical sessions will challenge you in creative and insightful ways. Use this video series with your family.

Includes the following:
- Thirteen 30-minute videos on 2 DVDs
- Kids Honor Club 13-session Children's Curriculum, 112 pages
- Say Goodbye to Whining, Complaining, and Bad Attitudes...in You and Your Kids book, 230 pages

To learn more give us a call or visit biblicalparenting.org

NATIONAL CENTER for BIBLICAL Parenting

76 Hopatcong Drive
Lawrenceville, NJ 08648-4136
Phone: (609) 771-8002
Email: parent@biblicalparenting.org

The Treasure Hunters

8-Session Children's Program Discovering God's Treasures in Family Life for Ages 3-12

Hidden within the common experiences of family life are treasures every child needs. Learning the value of correction, how to accept no as an answer, and the importance of a good attitude are important now but also for the future. Each of these eight lessons will help children ages 3-12 learn how to be more effective in their families. Use the Treasure Hunters Children's Curriculum in your Sunday School, during your Effective Parenting Support Group, or even in your own family. A vide-based parent training program is also available to complement this exciting children's program.

"Activity is the language of children. This curriculum communicates well to kids."

Posters are also available

To learn more give us a call or visit biblicalparenting.org

76 Hopatcong Drive
Lawrenceville, NJ 08648-4136
Phone: (609) 771-8002
Email: parent@biblicalparenting.org

Have Fun Teaching Children Spiritual Truths!

Six Activity Books
by Kirk Weaver

Family Time Activities Books

Each book contains fun, practical, and relevant ways to teach your children spiritual truths. Your kids will love them, but more importantly you'll build spiritual memories of Family Time in your home.

For All Ages
Energize your Family Time with science experiments, games, and activities that all teach spiritual lessons.

For Preschoolers
Preschoolers learn through games and play. These activities will teach them spiritual truths in fun ways.

For Teens
Teens need to be challenged to integrate values and convictions into life. These activities will help you do just that.

Books for all ages, for preschoolers, and for teens

To learn more give us a call or visit biblicalparenting.org

76 Hopatcong Drive
Lawrenceville, NJ 08648-4136
Phone: (609) 771-8002
Email: parent@biblicalparenting.org

Free
EMAIL PARENTING Tips

Receive guidance and inspiration a couple of times a week in your inbox.

Free Parenting Tips

Get practical suggestions to help you relate better to your kids and help your kids change their hearts, not just their behavior.

The tips are gleaned from the live seminars, books, and articles of Dr. Scott Turansky and Joanne Miller, RN, BSN. Here's what parents are saying about these short words of encouragement.

"We have a three year old and an eight year old, and so many tips apply to both. It's exciting for me when God delivers a tip on something we're struggling with and I'm able to share it with my husband. It get's conversation started and good things happen."

—mom of two, Wichita, KS

"Just wanted to let you know what a blessing your parenting tips have been to me and the others I share them with. I make copies of them to pass around and also save them on file. They truly help me and other parents learn practical and biblical principles of parenting."

—children's pastor, San Diego, CA

"These tips are very helpful and actually seem to come at a time when I need them. I have three teenagers ages 16, 14, and 13, so I always need help with something."

—mom of three, Ewing, NJ

To receive Free Email Parenting Tips sign up online at www.biblicalparenting.org or fill out the form at the left and mail. Also available in Spanish. Visit www.padresefectivos.org.

Sign up for free email parenting tips now. (You can remove yourself from the list at any time.) Your email address will not be shared or sold to others.

_____

Name

_____

Address

_____

City

_____

State   Zip

_____

Phone number with area code

_____

Email address

NATIONAL CENTER for BIBLICAL Parenting

76 Hopatcong Drive
Lawrenceville, NJ 08648-4136
(609) 771-8002
Email: parent@biblicalparenting.org
Web: biblicalparenting.org

Notes

Notes